DADVOTED

Dan,

So good to connect with you via LinkedIn. It's also rich to see your posts bathed in truth & scripture. I'm excited to share my book with you. My prayer is that this would challenge & change many men to live lives of purpose & substance so their kids will see the fruit of a life lived with purpose & substance!

DADVOTED

Dads Devoted to
Discovering their Duty,
Direction, and Destiny

KEVIN GOODNIGHT

XULON PRESS

Xulon Press
2301 Lucien Way #415
Maitland, FL 32751
407.339.4217
www.xulonpress.com

Paperback ISBN-13: 978-1-66287-436-9
Ebook ISBN-13: 978-1-66287-437-6

This book is dedicated to all dads regardless of what stage of life they find themselves in faith and fatherhood. The days are long, but the years are short. We only get one chance to live a life of purpose and substance so we can pass on a life of purpose and substance to the ones we've been entrusted to lead.

ACKNOWLEDGEMENTS

To King Jesus who reigns today. Who redeems, renews, and restores all who come to Him. Thank you for walking with and not giving up on me.

To my bride Keeli, who always saw great potential in me and loved me through every season. Thank you for your prayers and for journaling our journey. It's so rich to see how the Lord has orchestrated it all. And finally, thank you for making me a dad! I love you dearly.

To my boys Keaton and Kort, thank you for your sweet spirits and subtle nudges to write this book. My original prayer for this book was to create a family outline to pass on to you two and your future kids. May this book not only guide you in parenting one day, but always guide you in Christ as you discover your duty, direction and destiny.

CONTENTS

PRELUDE: MY JOURNEY

BECOMING A DAD is one of the most wonderful experiences you can have, but on the other hand is a very daunting undertaking. You thought your level of responsibility increased when you got married, but now you have another human whose precious life you are given the privilege to shape. Life becomes even less about you. Combine this newfound selflessness with the stage of life most of us are in at the time of becoming parents; your career is likely not off the ground, and you may still be trying to establish yourself and set your family up for success in the future. Merge your life circumstances together with the chaos that ensues once kids arrive, and you experience your new normal—which doesn't seem normal at all! How do you maintain intentionality when it comes to raising kids and teaching them life lessons?

I'll be the first to tell you that the past twelve years raising my boys has been a blur at times. I went through a massive career change seven years ago that stripped away many of my former freedoms. My family had to adapt to the pressure and stress of me running a business which also required commuting 95 miles a day in Houston, TX. There have been many ups and downs, but I couldn't have done it and maintained the same passion without my faith in Jesus and support from my wife, Keeli. I now pull in the driveway each day and say the same prayer: "Lord, give me the energy and strength to love on Keaton and Kort and be intentional with them."

The journey to writing this book has been interesting. I started well over a year ago making a list of topics on things I needed to teach my boys with the ultimate goal of raising them to become "great men of God." I feel, as most of you probably do, that this is the most important discipleship opportunity that God has given me. It is my great honor to guide, mold and shape them in such a way that they will live a life of substance and purpose with a focus on loving God and loving people. Easier said than done, right?

So, how did an outline or checklist turn into writing a book? At the beginning of the pandemic in 2020 I was woken in the middle of the night and heard the Lord speak to me. He said, "I'm going to show up big this year." I journaled this but really didn't press into it. The world was in shambles, my business was down, my employees were overworked, and everyone's incomes were affected in some way. The months during the pandemic were eerie as we didn't know what mandate was next around the corner, what surge was coming our way, or whether lockdown was near. There was turmoil everywhere you looked with so much hate and dissension in the world it was sickening. Believers had to worship "online," and the presence and peace of God seemed very distant.

On December 8th, 2020, I work up early and began journaling. The entry read:

"It's been eight months since my last entry, and I can say that going back and reading the early entries I have written here brings so much hope and excitement as I know the LORD is moving. Currently my back is against the wall. My business is down drastically, the promotion I was seeking was delayed (and ended up not happening) and a new boss who has a suspect history and managing method is on the attack against everything I have built. My sales manager is moving to Dallas leaving me a vacant position and there are so many errors lately that are affecting my sales team mentally, not to mention our sales as well.

I will admit that I have been in somewhat of a slumber over the past few months. I'm still working hard (or harder than ever), but I've been leaning on myself to fix things or escaping reality at night with a few cocktails. Ten days ago, I felt God's spirit of continued conviction to fast from alcohol to clear my mind and focus on a life driven by the Spirit. I am still trusting and leaning on the promise that I had earlier this year that God is going to show up big this year. I will say that the last ten days have been rich! My time with the Lord has been fulfilling. I am calmer, I'm sleeping better (once I fall asleep), and I have more energy at the end of the long work week. I like the way my mind, body and soul feel when I keep it clean. But all in all, my goal is to fast in obedience for preparation for the Lord to show up big. My plan is to continue to abstain from alcohol and seek Him fully! Right now, everything around me workwise looks bleak and concerning. I have a lot of work to do, and I feel that this season is a test (or maybe an attack), but either way, I'm going to persevere!!

Lord, thank you for your promises from scripture that help keep me grounded and I'm excited to see what is to come!"

- "Consider it pure joy when you face trials of many kinds" James 1:2-4
- God will move mountains – Isaiah 45
- Protection from the fire – Daniel 2
- "Be joyful in hope, patient in affliction, faithful in prayer" Rom 12:2
- "No weapon formed against me will prosper" Isiah 54:17
- "Whatever you do, work at it with all your heart, as working for the Lord and not for men" Col 3:23

I continued to press in over the next few weeks and then it happened. God showed up! He showed up BIG! On December 21ˢᵗ, 2020, I journaled the following:

"Last night, Keeli and I attended the wedding of her small group co-leader, Sofia. It was a beautiful ceremony and a fun party. Ironically, we were at a table with one other couple at dinner, where every other table was completely full. This couple happened to be prayer partners, and he was an elder at WoodsEdge (our home church). They were very cautious due to COVID and sat at the other end of the table as far as they could from us—add to that their thick Nigerian accent and masks made it very difficult to understand them over the music.

After dinner, we started to talk more about raising boys. They have two (ages 18 and 16), and we asked for any advice they had. They gave great advice on being patient, listening, accepting your kids and their friends, and of course praying like crazy. Towards the end of dinner, Tope, the wife, told Keeli that she felt that one day Keeli would write a children's book. From there, I told them about my vision from this year that God was going to show up big. Tope stopped and looked at me and said, "That's it!" "You are going to write a book about raising boys!" She had no clue that I had already started outlining that very book months ago. She confirmed that this was a prophecy from the Lord and that it would be done to glorify God and further the Kingdom.

Wow!! Was that dinner outing just a coincidence? Absolutely not! That was a divine meeting arranged by the Lord to confirm God's vision and direction for me and our family. I don't know what this means, but I guess I am officially an author for the Lord!

God, thank You for Your guidance, direction, and vision for my life. This has been such a tough and interesting season and I must admit that I have had many moments of doubt and disobedience. But Your love is so good, never waivers, is consistent and strong. Father, I don't know where to start in this journey other than jumping right in and trusting You! Lord, continue to pour out Your grace and spirit on me. Thank You for Sam and Tope and our divine dinner last night. Continue to put people in my life like them to guide and direct me. Thank You for Your gift of writing You have given me. May it bless many and turn more people to You!"

Reading back through these journal entries brings up a ton of emotions, and I'm excited to share these thoughts with you. Though we will touch base on many ideas for raising kids, the main premise of this book is to challenge dads to discover their duty, direction and destiny as a parent. Though I'm no trained expert – I'm in the trenches raising my boys right now – I hope this book provides a solid baseline and helps create the intentionality that is vital in the endeavor dads have been given. This book is split into three sections. Section one is foundational in nature, challenging dads to build a strong foundation to be able to tackle anything. Section two is more practical in nature, as we address topics that we face today that we may or may not be prepared for. The third section concludes with a charge to all dads. My wife, Keeli, will also contribute a lot of uncited insight to the book as she's much calmer and smarter and is usually at the forefront of the hardest posed questions by our kids.

The ultimate goal of parenting is to plant seeds of greatness in your kids, water them with truth and point them to God so He can grow them for His purpose and for the betterment of our society. I hope you enjoy and are challenged as you grow in your Dadvotedness.

DADVOTED?

FIRST AND FOREMOST, let me set the record straight: this is not a political literary piece explaining how this dad voted or how you should vote. You will not get an ounce of political rhetoric out of me, or at least any that will sway you to the left or the right. Dadvoted stems from the words "dad" and "devoted." So, what does this mean? When I right click on devoted in Word, I get the following synonyms:

Dedicated, Enthusiastic, Staunch, Fervent, Loving

Dedicated: When you are devoted to something, you dedicate everything in your power to see it succeed. You are laser focused. You are All In! There's no wavering. There's no wishy-washy behavior. There's no quitting. Being Dadvoted incapsulates all these characteristics to the fullest. You are committed to seeing your kids grow and develop with the goal of having them give back and contribute to the betterment of society. You set their direction and help them along the path of life. There are no days off!

Enthusiastic: When you are devoted, you embody excitement. It oozes out of every pore. Not everyone understands the "why," but they respect your "why." You yearn for greatness in a healthy manner and navigate issues and problems, as you know that this is part of the process. Being Dadvoted naturally brings enthusiasm with it. It's engrained in you. You face problems head on and don't run from them. You are strong, bold, and courageous. Everything you do is for the greater good of your kids. You make the tough decisions even when that decision isn't popular with what everyone else is saying or doing.

Staunch: Staunch is an adjective meaning loyal and committed in attitude. "Strongly built and firm construction" falls into secondary definitions. (Oxford Dictionaries).[1] Those who are Dadvoted are loyal and committed in attitude. They are helping to build a strong foundation in their kids' lives that will withstand any test, trial, or storm. They teach them that they won't always get their way and sometimes that is for the best. They stand next to their kids in both victory and defeat. They are selfless and give up comforts or even bigger opportunities that don't add value to the future of the kids.

Fervent: Fervent is described as "Passionate Intensity." (Oxford Dictionaries)[2] Wow! I've been called passionate a time or two – sometimes for both good and bad – and have been noted as having a high level of intensity, but "passionate intensity" is a phrase I've never seen combined. Being devoted means that you have the highest level of passionate intensity to the cause you are championing. So, being Dadvoted means exactly that. You are championing the raising of kids to become great and to do that requires passionate intensity.

Loving: Loving may appear to pivot from that of the other 4 words, and to some may weaken the meaning of being devoted, but I disagree. If you are devoted, you are a big lover. You are understanding and caring. You are tender, but you also tell the truth and don't sugarcoat. That is the same of being Dadvoted. You care deeply. You pick up and dust off your kids when they are hurt or wronged. You speak the truth to them, but in love. Even on the hard topics or when they are wrong. You protect, but you don't overprotect. You correct, but you don't overcorrect. Sometimes you let them fail so that they learn. But you are always there!

What I love most about the five synonyms above is the order they came in. I did not adjust this order but pulled them exactly how they fell in the list. These five words couldn't have been placed in a better order if I tried it myself. Dedicated, Enthusiastic, Staunch, Fervent, Loving. The starting place of "Dedicated" and the ending place of "Loving" are the best bookends for the three more emotional words in the middle: Enthusiastic, Staunch and Fervent. It all starts with Dedication and ends with Love. That's what being Dadvoted is all about.

Some of you might not have had a Dadvoted father growing up or had an only partially Dadvoted father in your youth and that's okay. That doesn't define who *you* are as a dad. If you have gotten this far, you have done the hardest part of committing to the greater good of raising your kids. It's not too late. Much of this book is going to reference and pull from the most Dadvoted father of all, and that is God. When I look at the life of Jesus, the five synonyms of being devoted describe Him to the fullest and more importantly how He views us. He cares deeply for us, with immense loyalty, passionate intensity, dedication, commitment, and love. He cares even more than we can imagine or understand; even when we don't love Him back, waiver in our faith, or live disobediently. I know we are all on different spiritual journeys right now and that also is okay. Wherever you land today, I hope you know that God loves you deeply and wants not only the best for you, but for your kids and He's ready to partner with you today! You already have everything engrained in you to be fully Dadvoted. It's ready to be unleashed and the time is now!

SECTION 1:
FOUNDATION BUILDING

DUTY, DIRECTION
AND DESTINY

WHAT COMES INTO your mind when I say triple d's? Ok, maybe that's a bad question for guys. My mind goes right to *Diners, Drive-ins and Dives* as I love to eat at local joints and live from meal to meal, often thinking about my lunch when I am eating my breakfast and so on and so forth. Maybe that's not where your mind went at all (shame on you). Duty, direction and destiny are the most important triple d's we dads need to be focusing on. Maybe you are, maybe you aren't, or like a lot of us you are just trying to keep your head above water in this mad race of life that we are trying to figure out. I'm with you. Let's take a deep breath and see if we are in line, need to adjust, or need a full pivot on these three most important topics.

Duty – What key words describe our duty as men? I tend to think of responsibilities, obligations and jobs. As a dad, the lists of tasks are almost endless. We have numerous responsibilities at home: raising kids, paying bills, being a good husband, fixing things (or in my case, writing checks to have things fixed), electric bills, phone bills, water bills, yardwork, keeping the house clean, paying taxes, car maintenance, budgeting, saving for college, being a good husband (yes, repeated on purpose), playing with your kids, helping with homework, cooking (yes you can), grocery shopping (you should try it), doing the bedtime routine, and finally being a good husband (yes, repeated again for emphasis). This list is only partial in nature but is exhausting. By the way, your wife's list would run for a few more pages, so we don't have it so bad. I won't venture into the work side of life as that list is just as daunting to say the least. When people ask me what I do for a living, I just say that I run an adult daycare. You may feel my pain as well.

Either way, we have so much noise in our lives; so many obligations and a ton of hats to wear. We find it hard to set a plan and stick to it, because there are so many other things vying for our time, energy and attention. I'm going to narrow it down today in hopes to take the burden off you. Dadvoted men reading right now, let's focus on being really good at three things:

1. **Loving Jesus**

2. **Out serving our wife**

3. **Being intentional with our kids**

If you can quiet all the noise and really focus on these 3 things, the rest will fall into place. You notice that there is nothing here about being a banner employee and giving your all to your career. I did this intentionally as I say that falls under loving Jesus. If you love Jesus, you will "work as if you are working for the Lord" (Colossians 3:23). The balance of this book will in some way, form, or fashion relate back to all 3 of these topics. Let's get out of the weeds so we can love big, have joy regardless of what is thrown our way and be the dads we were made to be.

Direction – Are you pointed in the right direction now? Do you have goals, dreams and ambitions? I hope so. Here is the challenging question: are those goals, dreams and ambitions part of God's will for your life? Or are they selfish in nature? Are they rooted in the desire to please God or in the desire to please yourself? Are they moving in a direction that you are giving, or are they wired with the ultimate goal of you getting; getting more money, stuff, accolades, titles, bigger, faster, more, more, more. These are tough questions; indeed, I've been there and sometimes revert back and have to reset. I'm not sitting here telling you that if your goals don't line up with God's purpose that they won't come true. God may still bless you and have them come to fruition. But what I will emphasize is that if your goals, dreams and ambitions don't line up with God's will and purpose for your life, you will never be fully satisfied in your work. I challenge you to read Ecclesiastes this week, one chapter at a time. Right out the gate the writer states:

"Meaningless! Meaningless! Utterly meaningless! Everything is meaningless" (Ecclesiastes 1:2.)

Then in in chapter 2 verses 22-26 it says, "A person can do nothing better than to eat and drink and find satisfaction in their own toil. This too, I see, is from the hand of God, for without Him who can eat or find enjoyment? To the person who pleases Him, God gives wisdom, knowledge and happiness, but to the sinner He gives the task of gathering and storing up wealth to hand it over to the one who pleases God. This too is meaningless, a chasing after the wind."

So, how do you know if you are headed in the right direction in life and in your career? If you are rooted and grounded in Christ, full of faith, seeking God in all decisions, and worshipping him wholeheartedly, you are on a good path. Next to that, the biggest internal test is centered around your prayer life. Do you pray often? Are you desperately seeking God? Not just the favor of God, but the face of God. Meeting with Him daily to soak in His love for you and humbly calling on Him in all situations is key.

Regarding your career, I can't answer that for you. I do know that God needs more Godly men in the marketplace. Your job should be part of your ministry, pointing people to Christ through your words and actions. I understand that this can be dicey but step out in faith. People need to be encouraged and uplifted. You as a believer, with Christ living in you, have the keys to answer any question. Also, how you act at work shouldn't be different than how you act outside of work. Don't be someone different at work to try and fit in to the culture of that company. If you feel stuck in a career, seek the Lord for wisdom, guidance and direction. He will show up, I promise. Every large career move I've ever made has been bathed in prayer and the direction has been so obvious as whether to take the job, pass on the job, leave the company or stay with the company. Every time! Two of my major job moves took place when my wife was pregnant. That led me to get a vasectomy after the second time as I couldn't risk another major life change taking place simultaneously for the third time! At the end of the day, I'm not smart enough on my own to make major decisions without the best guidance one can get and that comes from God.

Destiny – Destiny comes in two forms—your fate or destination when you die and your purpose while you live. I hope you can sense early on that I am assuming you are a believer in Jesus and that my goal is to help fine-tune you to become the best version of yourself so that you can understand and live in God's purpose for you. If you think I'm off my rocker regarding Jesus and salvation, that's okay as well, but I won't sugarcoat that there is a fate that we will all one day face. If you are uncertain or don't know where you are going when that happens, I challenge you to begin a path of uncovering your destiny or final destination when your short time on Earth is completed. God has promised the gift of eternal life with Him in heaven to those who put their hope, faith and trust in Jesus.

John 14:1-4 states this so beautifully when Jesus says, "Do not let your hearts be troubled. You believe in God; believe also in me. My Father's house has many rooms; if that were not so, would I have told you that I am going there to prepare a place for you? And if I go and prepare a place for you, I will come back and take you to be with me that you also may be where I am. You know the way to the place where I am going."

I love how this verse says, "You believe in God; believe also in me." A lot of people believe in God. In fact, a lot of religions believe in God. Even the demons believe in God (James 2:19). The dividing line is that of Jesus; that Jesus was both fully man and fully God and that He came to earth to rescue His people. A lot of religions believe that Jesus walked the earth and was a good teacher, but that He wasn't the Messiah. The way to heaven is through Jesus.

The flipside to Heaven is that there is Hell. Hell isn't talked about very much. It's a tough topic. How would this loving God allow people to suffer for eternity in Hell? That's a tough question and I'm no theologian, but here is what I know. The Bible doesn't sugarcoat this either. There will be judgement. We must all give an account of the short life we lived on earth. Philippians 3:18-21 gives a quick snapshot of Heaven and Hell:

"For, as I have often told you before and now tell you again even with tears, many live as enemies of the cross of Christ. Their destiny is destruction, their god is their stomach, and their glory is their shame. Their mind is set on earthly things. But our citizenship is in heaven. And we eagerly await a Savior from there, the Lord Jesus Christ, who by the power that enables him to bring everything under control, will transform our lowly bodies so that they will be like his glorious body."

Paul is writing this not only as a warning. He is burdened by the thought, so much so that he is in tears. Honest question here, do you feel this way about the people you know and love that don't know and love Jesus? I certainly need to check myself here. Next, he says that "their <u>destiny</u> is destruction." That is their end. And the three things that accompany them are:

"<u>Their god is their stomach</u>" – Their appetite is what they seek to serve. It's all about pleasure. If it feels good, do it is their mantra.

"<u>Their glory is their shame</u>" – They brag about the dark things they do. They think it brings them glory. You've seen it. Men talking about sexual escapades and conquests. Stories on binge drinking, etc.

"<u>Their mind is set on earthly things</u>" – It's all about them, them, them. And what they can gain and obtain. Living for self.

Dadvoted reader, I can't convince you with my words that both heaven and hell exist. You must go on this journey for yourself if you don't know. I pray if you are on the fence or unsure, that you seek to find the answer through asking God and finding a biblical church. Also, it doesn't matter how far gone you are and what bad you have done. God is waiting for you. You must call upon Him and He will show up, forgive you and give you a new life. From there you must stay the course and live for Him.

The second part of your destiny is your future or purpose here while on Earth. Once you are secure in your final destination, you must uncover your earthly purpose. Not a lot of men know their purpose. Even believers. As dads, there is no doubt in my mind that our #1 purpose is to raise our kids with a knowledge of God and disciple them towards living a life for Jesus. But we can't stop there. God has an even larger calling for each one of us as believers to help advance His Kingdom. We've got to uncover this purpose.

We've got to unlock this purpose. We've got to unleash this purpose! After discussing how you get saved through grace in Ephesians 2:8-9 verse 10 then says; "For we are God's handiwork, created in Christ Jesus to do good works, which <u>God prepared in advance for us to do</u>." Jeremiah 29:11 says, "For I know the plans I have for you," declares the Lord, "plans to prosper you and not harm you, plans to give you hope and a future." The God that created the universe with His mere words, also created you and created you to do something big. So how do you uncover this? I think that's the million-dollar question here. I don't know of any section in the Bible that gives you the easy answer, so I'll walk you through my journey in hopes that you can mimic or find parallels to help you in yours.

First, I don't think that God is just going to dump a purpose on you in one fail swoop. Maybe so, but He didn't for me. If you read the prelude at the beginning of this book, you see that God woke me in the middle of the night and said, "I'm going to show up big for you this year." Then nothing happened for months. Thankfully I journaled this and remembered it. I prayed over it here and there but didn't yearn for this promise until December when I realized that the year was almost up. I fasted from alcohol to clear my mind as I believe that fasting supercharges your prayer life and perks God up as He sees you are committed and expecting Him to move. Another week and a half passed and nothing happened. Then, we attended the wedding and God orchestrated a divine meeting (as only He can do) where a lady spoke over me saying I was going to write a book. This drives home another point; if it sounds outrageous, it is even more likely to be from God. I'm not an author. I feel that I communicate well via written word, but never pictured myself writing a book. I now not only have this book, but two others in the works—crazy! The story of God revealing a new identity to me is for a later entry, but my purpose and identity are linked, and even though I consider myself crafty with words and marketing, I could have never come up with this on my own. This solidifies even more so that it was from God and not from me.

Breakdown for uncovering your purpose

- Humbly approach God to begin revealing your purpose to you through prayer and reading His Word
- Don't expect it to come all at once, but in small chunks that you must formulate and piece together
- Eliminate blatant sin in your life so your prayer life isn't hindered
- Fasting supercharges God's movement
- If something off the wall is revealed to you, don't pass it off but press in. It if doesn't make sense, chances are it is probably from God.
- Don't let fear creep in, pray against the enemy stripping your purpose away
- Journal it – also reveal it to a close friend or spouse who knows the Lord
- God's timing, not your timing – God gave me an approximate timeline, but didn't give me specifics
- Once revealed, obedience is required – Don't delay or overthink it like I did. Take steps of faith immediately.
- Tell your close circle of friends so they can encourage you and keep you accountable

Dadvoted reader, God doesn't need you to move His Kingdom, but He wants you. He wants you to live a life of freedom devoted to Him. When you have your God given purpose realizing that the same power that created the universe and raised Christ from the dead lives inside of you, you are unstoppable! There is no room for fear. No room to acknowledge the naysayers. You walk with confidence and a bounce in your step, knowing that God's promises come true. I can't wait to hear your stories of purpose being revealed. Email me at dadvoted@gmail.com so these can be shared to encourage many. You were made for purpose and adventure. Don't let your one life pass you by without unlocking and living this out!

GOD IS REAL, GOD IS GOOD, GOD IS KING

LIVING IN THE bible belt in Texas, many people seem to know without question that God is real. Almost all the people I know grew up with a basic knowledge that God created the heavens and the earth, man and woman, and sent His son Jesus to die for us. This basic knowledge is where a lot of us start as we begin to teach our children with the help of Bible stories and Sunday school. And of course, the answer to every "church question" is Jesus. As parents it is extremely important to teach our kids the Bible stories and the "basics" to build a foundation for their life. But what is our motivation? Is it to build up morally "good" kids? What is your parental foundation? Do we believe that the God of the universe who created the galaxy with His words is still real and working today? Do we believe that He knit your child in the womb (Psalm 139:13) and has major plans for each one of your children for the kingdom (Jer 29:11)? If you don't believe that God is real and is working today, and you just happened to get this book to become a better dad for raising your kids or someone gifted you this book, that is okay as well. My challenge for you would be to seek God in prayer and ask Him if He is real. Then, open a Bible, dive in, and find a local church that believes and teaches the Bible. Proverbs 8:17 says, "I love those who love me, and those who seek me find me." There is no better time than now!

Next, do you believe that God is good? A lot of us grew up in strict rule-based religion and learned more about the "dos and don'ts" rather than about a loving relationship with our Savior. In the opening sentence of his book *The Knowledge of the Holy,* A.W. Tozer said, "What comes into your minds when we think about God is the most important thing about us." (Tozer, 1978)[3] What comes into your mind when you think about God? Do you picture a task master? Do you picture someone who is here to take away all the fun things? Do you picture someone waiting for you to mess up so you can be punished? If so, let me tell you that the God of the Bible is not this God. He is a tender, loving father who wants the best for you and for your kids. He wants to protect your life and use it for good. His promises are rich and include the best promise – that of eternal life for every person that puts their hope, faith, and trust in Jesus. I'm also sensitive to the fact that a lot of us didn't grow up with a solid earthly father, and I can imagine that this makes it difficult for some of us to trust a Heavenly Father. Trust me please! He is good, He is good, He is good.

Do you believe that God is King? That He is the King of the universe and everything in it. Do you believe that He reigns supreme on His throne? Do you believe that one day King Jesus is coming back? Maybe the ultimate question is this: what or who is acting as king in your life right now? What consumes you? Is it your job? Is it the next promotion? Is it pleasing people? Is it keeping up with the Joneses? Is it your kids (ouch!) and their activities? I know this is deep stuff right out of the gate, and I still fight the same battles, but this early entry is more or less a challenge and encouragement to all the dads reading. If you don't believe that God is real, God is good, and God is King, I want to challenge you to evaluate and do a self-check—and don't throw this book away! Billy Graham said it best late in his life when he quoted, "Life without God is like an unsharpened pencil – it has no point." *(Diasover, 2009)*[4]

Let's be honest. We are never fully prepared to parent. Parenting today is tougher than ever, especially with all the access to technology we and our children have at our fingertips. We are busier than ever. We are tired. We are running a rat race that leads nowhere. It doesn't have to be this way. We have eighteen long but short years to raise our kids and point them toward God. But that starts with us as parents. We must be present. We must be intentional. We must lean on God's word and promises. We must meet with Him daily for guidance, direction, and wisdom. Otherwise, we are going to let the world raise our kids. We only have one shot, one chance to impart the things of God in their lives. Let's be ALL in!

NEVER GOOD ENOUGH

THESE ARE WORDS that none of us want to hear. This is also a statement that has driven some of the greatest to reach heights never thought attainable. Michael Jordan was cut from his high school basketball team. Kurt Warner was cut early in his career by the Green Bay Packers and had to take a job stocking shelves at a local grocery store. Both of those men used the rejection as fuel to ignite them to become great. Personally, I still use a comment from a competitor telling me that I would "only last one year" in this business as fuel to wake up every day and compete to dominate. Ironically that same person told me the same thing in the second year as well. I'm now into year seven. By no means am I comparing myself to MJ or two-time MVP and Super Bowl MVP Kurt Warner, but being told I'd never be good enough to compete long term in the industry that I chose (and the Lord directed me to) has been helpful to keep me on track when I get down on myself or encounter setbacks.

Men don't like being told that they are never going to be good enough. Well, I'm going to flip the script today and tell you that you will never be good enough in God's eyes. Hold the press! You are saying that the all-knowing, loving, redeeming God will never think I'm good enough? I think that's what I'm saying. Let me break it down. We live in a world where you have to earn everything. Very little is given to you. You work hard, you tirelessly strain to obtain. So, when it comes to your salvation, the natural thought is that you have to earn it or work hard to get it. That is not the case. Your salvation is given to you once you put your faith in Jesus. It doesn't cost you anything as it's a free gift. Dadvoted reader, I want you to absorb this statement for a second. There is nothing you can do to make God love you more, and nothing you can do to make God love you less.

The word for this is grace. Grace is the key factor between Christianity and every other religion out there. This may be one of the hardest things for men to grasp as we are all about performance. I love how God's word smashes the performance concept. It says, "for it is by grace you have been saved, through faith – and this is not from yourselves, it is the gift of God – not by works, so that no one can boast" (Ephesians 2: 8-9). Pretty clearly written and stated, you cannot earn your way into Heaven. You have an equal chance as anyone to be accepted into God's Kingdom. There is not a scale waiting for you at the pearly gates, with all your good deeds on one side of it and your bad on the other. Many people and religions think that if your good outweighs your bad you get in. We could never be good enough to pass that test in God's eyes. In fact, God says, "all our righteous acts are like filthy rags" (Isaiah 64:6). Not to gross you out, but filthy rags in early bible times refers to the saying "on the rag," or a woman's period. So, are our best acts are considered on the same level as that? Pretty much.

This shouldn't discourage you from doing good things, but is more a comparison for those on the performance plan trying to win God's favor. In James 2, the Bible says, "faith without deeds is dead." We should strive to do good once we become a believer, but that is to promotes God's name, not to gain entry into Heaven. I hope that all of this encourages you to get off the religious treadmill, where you are trying so hard, but not going anywhere at all. In Titus 3:5 (ESV) the Bible reiterates all of this by saying, "He saved us, not because of works done by us in righteousness, but according to His own mercy, by the washing of regeneration and renewal of the Holy Spirit." This should be good news to you. In fact, the Gospel, or Jesus coming and dying for us to save us, is called "Good News." Religion is about doing; the Gospel says it's already been done! Christ paid the ultimate price for us on the cross.

Dadvoted reader, get off the performance plan and join the grace plan. Accept God's gift of salvation. In faith, know that Jesus came to Earth to save and rescue you from sin and gifted you with eternal life. Accept it. Live in it. Be changed by it. Once you have that established, you should be changed. How you think, act and feel should be different. You are now on God's team, and your only working should be working for Him to advance His will and purpose for your life to reach others.

"I DON'T MAKE MISTAKES!"

WHEN MY FIRSTBORN, Keaton, was young, he was attached to his mom, as are many boys. He spent the most time with her and developed a deep connection. This story isn't unique by any means. As he began to walk and grow, he began to mirror the activities of Keeli and wanted to be "pretty" like Mom. This included wanting to put on her makeup, wear her jewelry, walk around in her high heels, and do other things that are feminine in nature. This didn't bother me at first, as he was little and again, I believe this isn't off-the-wall activity for a little boy. Unfortunately, I let the lies of the enemy creep in through people I won't name, telling me that Keaton was different and that I needed to fix this and "man him up." I became very sensitive to his activities, often stepping in to end his behavior. This really bothered me, and I don't remember talking about it with Keeli. If I did, she most likely told me not to worry about it.

At that time, we were in a small group at our church with some close friends who we had been doing life with for a few years. At one of our gatherings, instead of ending in normal prayer with requests and praying over each other, Krista, our group leader, said she wanted to engage in listening prayer. I might have heard of this form of prayer, but I had never actively embarked in listening prayer to my knowledge. To set the stage, she said, "I want us to spend a moment with Jesus. I want you to picture yourself in a peaceful setting sitting next to Jesus and soaking up His love for you. After that,

I want you to ask Him if there is anything he wants to say to you. From there, just clear your mind and listen."

We all closed our eyes and I pictured myself sitting under a weeping willow tree next to a beautiful river. I didn't know it at the time, but Keeli and I have now come to love this very river over the past few years. I picture Psalm 1 when I think about the river:

"Blessed is the one who does not walk in step with the wicked or stand in the way that sinners take or sit in the company of mockers, but whose delight is in the law of the Lord and who meditates on his law day and night. That person is like a tree planted by streams of water, which yields its fruit in season and whose leaf does not whither – whatever they do prospers." Psalm 1:1-3

To me, the river is calming and nurturing but it can also be powerful and overtake us. I also picture Jesus the same way. He is calm and nurturing but also powerful and can overtake us. Now, back to the listening prayer experience. I sat next to Jesus under this beautiful weeping willow tree, next to a smooth-running turquoise river (most likely the Guadalupe) and I began to soak in His love for me for a few minutes. I then told Jesus that I was concerned about Keaton and that he was different. Before I could even ask Him to speak to me, I immediately–in a strong, firm, booming voice–heard Jesus tell me, "I don't make mistakes!" Wow! I had only heard Jesus audibly a few times, but this was like no other. It was a powerful voice that I imagine He will use one day to proclaim to the world that He's back to get His people. It made me shutter and shiver and was like nothing I had ever heard before. Yet, this was also calming and confirmed that God created my child and that he was perfect in His eyes.

I want to encourage you today that whatever stage in life your child is in, they are fearfully and wonderfully made by God (Psalm

139:14). Regardless of what they are doing, have done, or will do, they are perfect in God's sight because God doesn't make mistakes!

A GOOD NAME

PROVERBS 22:1 SAYS, "A good name is more desirable than great riches; to be esteemed is better than silver or gold." Another way to put this sentiment is that to be respected and admired is greater and more valuable than the greatest wealth. How do we instill this in our kids? I don't think this is a one-time conversation, but an ongoing conversation with them throughout all the different stages of life they are going through. It starts with teaching your kids that to be respected, they must first respect themselves. That they need to choose their friends wisely and the decisions they make can affect them for the rest of their lives. These conversations can be subtle through their early years to build a base foundation, but as they grow and get into middle school and high school, they must be had in a real manner and repeated often.

Maybe the simplest way to explain this is to take your kids out to a local football field. The field is 100 yards in length. Let this represent the number of years in their life (or at least the goal for most of us). Then go stand on the 13-yard line and walk to the 18-yard line. Explain that these five yards represent their teenage years in middle school and high school. Then have them look all the way down the field to the opposite goal line. Compare these five yards to the remaining 82 yards. This shows them how small of a window these years are compared to the rest of their life. Explain to them that bad decisions made during this short window of time can affect them forever. Give specific examples of things that can happen. It's your call how intense you take the conversation, but we all know people that suffered extreme consequences from bad decisions made during this vital time in their lives; from unplanned pregnancies, to drinking and driving and drug use that leads to years of addition, and even decisions that ended fatally. They need to understand that these things are real and do happen and we've seen it firsthand. I've also seen God redeem these situations, but our hope and prayer for our children is that we don't want these situations redeemed but that they never happen. We must be intentional and have these conversations.

I remember being in eighth grade at a track meet and was offered to go under the bleachers and smoke pot. It was sold to me as no big deal and that no one would find out. Four of my buddies decided to go do this. All of them were athletes except the guy offering, and thought they were untouchable and that no one would tell. The very next week, they all got called in and expelled from eighth grade for the balance of the year and had to go to alternative school. They all had to plea with the administrative staff to let them into high school and not continue down the alternative school route for high school, which would have greatly affected their chances of getting into college. They were embarrassed, their families were ashamed, and this followed them for many years. I was so close to saying yes and joining them, but thankfully opted out. That decision could have greatly altered my life.

I urge you to read Proverbs 22 as there are so many rich passages that relate to raising your kids. As a parent, Proverbs 22:6 says the most to me: "Start children off on the way they should go, and when they are old they will not turn from it."

Dadvoted reader, your child's name and reputation matters. We can't turn from these conversations or hope that we are good, because we have a good kid. Don't be naïve, don't hope for the best. You play a huge role in shaping your kids.

If your child has already gone down a wrong path or is headed that way, pray for God's redeeming love to show up and redirect your child. There are so many comeback stories in the Bible for you to lean on during this time to give you hope like the prodigal son in Luke 15:11-32. Seek God. Plea to the Lord and He will hear your cry!

LIFE VERSE

AS WE SEARCH to impart truth into the young hearts we are raising, I find it vital to bathe our kids in scripture repeatedly. One way we have found this to be easier to achieve was to give each one of our boys a verse that we have printed on their wall so they can see it and we can pray it over them at night. This is an easy and refreshing way to speak truth over them and encourage them often. Also, we are not immune from the rest of the parents out there that are absolutely whooped after a long day and must fight the night-time routine. Keeli will not be happy with me saying this, but most of her meltdowns (which are few and far between) seem to come in the last five minutes of the day when all her energy has been spent and given to these knuckleheads and she is ready for her own time. I digress but want to encourage you to seek the Lord for verses that you can publish on their wall in any fashion you want. I also want to share my boy's verses as well:

~KEATON'S PRAYER~

"Since the day we first heard about you,
we have not stopped praying for you.
We continually ask God to fill you with
the knowledge of his will through all the
wisdom and understanding that the Spirit
gives, so that you may live a life worthy
of the Lord and please him in every way."

COLOSSIANS 1:9-10

~KORT'S PRAYER~

"I pray that from his glorious, unlimited
resources the Lord will empower you with
inner strength through his spirit. Then
Christ will make his home in your heart
as you trust in him. Your roots will grow
down into God's love and keep you strong.'

EPHESIANS 3:16-17

A few years ago, I took this a step further. I came across 1 Corinthians 16: 13-14 and I decided to make this the life verse for both me and my boys. I wrote this on February 10th, 2020. To refresh your memory, this was at the height of some of the hardest times I've seen in America. Politically the United States was more divided than ever after the election. Racial injustice had skyrocketed as well as social injustice. I had never seen so much hatred in the world. The COVID-19 pandemic was close to fully making its way here and I was overall just sad for our country. I wrote the following to my boys, read it to them before school in tears and then Keeli printed and framed this and put it in their rooms:

> **1 Corinthians 16:13-14**
> **Be on guard; stand firm in the faith; be men of courage; be strong. Do everything in love.**
>
> Lord, I pray this verse over me, Keaton and Kort. This verse spells out what a true man is. There is no fear, guilt, shame, anxiety or condemnation in you!
>
> We are on guard! We recognize the schemes of the enemy and laugh at them. We stand firm in You when the world tries to bring us down or drag us away. We have courage to do what is right and to protect the weak. We are strong mentally, spiritually and physically with discipline and self-control that is derived from You. Finally, we love and respect all people regardless of where they are from. We love and respect women and we are always pointing people to You, our Savior who loved us first!
>
> Walk in Obedience & Run to Jesus
>
> Love, Dad
>
> 2-10-2020

To me this verse epitomizes what it is to be a true man of God.

Be on guard – There are so many things out to get us, both seen and unseen in the forms of people, worldly and demonic. People are out for themselves. Some will lie, cheat, and use you to get ahead. We must have discernment with our personal interactions. I also lean on 1 Peter 1:12 that says: "Live such good lives among the pagans that, though they accuse you of doing wrong, they may see your good deeds and glorify God on the day he visits us." We can't control other people's actions; all we can control is our *reactions*. I am by no means telling you to teach your kids not to trust people, but to be on guard and to seek God for discernment.

Worldly enemies are harder to decipher, because we are subtly exposed to so much through advertising and social media and have unfortunately become numb to many threats. A few examples of worldly enemies include the drive and desire to get as much stuff as we can. And that we are never happy until we have X, until we make X amount of money, until we marry this person, or until we divorce that person. The world has shifted big time over the past 40 years as to what is acceptable and what is not. The believer is becoming the outcast and will continue to suffer higher levels of social persecution, at least in the United States, if not worse in the coming years. We as believers must be different than the world if we want to influence our kids and shift the culture.

Demonic enemies are a little more difficult to explain or harder for most of us to wrap our brains around. There is a real spiritual battle out there and we must be aware, vigilant, and not aloof about it. The Bible references this many times, but the 2 that come to mind are:

Ephesians 6:12
"For our struggle is not against flesh and blood,
but against the rulers, against the authorities,
against the powers of this dark world and against
the spiritual forces of evil in the heavenly realms."

1 Peter 5:8
"Be self-controlled and alert. Your enemy the
devil prowls around like a roaring lion looking for
someone to devour."

I will speak more of this later, but we must be aware, arm ourselves and go on the attack.

Stand firm in the faith – "Faith is being sure of what we hope for and certain of what we do not see." (Hebrews 11:1) As men of God we are sure and certain of a couple of things.

First, that when we put our hope and trust in Jesus that He saves us and gives us eternal life immediately. Second, that Jesus is coming back one day to judge all of creation. Third, that we will be with Him in eternity forever and there is nothing that can take that away.

Not everyone believes this or lives with this type of hope. We stand firm in it. It is the root of every decision that we make. We don't waiver. Our faith is our backbone, our main reason for the joy and peace we have amongst all the chaos in the world.

Be men of courage – Men of courage stand up for what is right no matter what. They don't conform to the world or to what is popular. They aren't bullies nor do they allow bullies to take over. They respect women, those who are weak, different, or those in need. They don't back down from what is right. They don't retreat. They protect.

Be strong – I don't think this speaks to physical strength as much as it speaks to mental and spiritual strength. But improving our mental and spiritual strength is similar to increasing our physical strength in a couple of ways. First, you must work on it. To build muscles, you exercise consistently. You mix up your workout so that your body doesn't become accustomed to the same routine. This is the same for the mental and spiritual battle. You must work on it consistently in a combination of routines that include prayer and bible time, meeting with like-minded believers to establish accountability, finding a mentor that can guide you through life, and serving in different capacities.

Second, like building physical strength, to build mental and spiritual strength there is some sort of pain or discomfort involved. You get up earlier to meet with Jesus and not sleep in. You choose to abstain from certain pleasures and yearn for more self-control. You say no to some of your friends that have been known to pull you away. And you may have to put yourself out there and ask someone to mentor you or join a men's group by yourself.

Do everything in love – Jesus left us with the two greatest commandments in Matt 22: 36-40. "Teacher, which is the greatest commandment in the Law?" Jesus replied: "Love the Lord your God with all your heart and with all your soul and with all your mind. And the second is like it: Love your neighbor as yourself. All the Law and the Prophets hang on these two commandments."

Men of God love big. Their first love is Jesus. They soak in His love daily so that it exudes out to everyone around them. They are compassionate. They are empathic. They aren't afraid to show their emotions. They serve. They are selfless. They are humble.

To my Dadvoted reader. I know life is hard. We have stress; we are busy and overwhelmed at times. One of our greatest missions and purpose on this Earth for the short time we get is to raise our kids to seek the things of God so they can influence the world in a major way. I encourage you to take small steps today to point them to Jesus and it starts with scripture. Pray for Jesus to reveal a life verse to you or a family verse. Display it in your home. Talk about it with your kids. Press into praying for them and over them. This will be richly rewarded one day, somehow. Be intentional. I hope you sense my passion and eagerness. I to let too much time go by and I only have a few years left before my boys leave this house and go out into the world. We are in charge of building the firm foundation on which our kids will live on for the rest of their lives.

"RUN TO JESUS"

IN MY PRAYER letter to my boys, I closed with walk in obedience and "Run to Jesus." I want to expand on the "Run to Jesus" quote and honor the person that gave me these words. To date, creating this entry has come with the greatest amount of writer's block as I don't know where to start and moreover how to give the justice deserved to the beautiful soul that spoke these words, which ended up being some of her last.

My best friend's wife, Christina, entered into an extremely tough battle with stage 4 colon and liver cancer through a hereditary gene called F.A.P. at the age of 33. She knew about this gene at an early age as she witnessed her father pass away due to the same complications. She didn't know if she would ever come down with cancer and if so at what age, as doctors didn't have solid information other than the knowledge to monitor it. She just knew that she had the gene and there was a future chance of cancer at some point.

We met them in our small group and instantly I had a connection with Chris. He was a huge personality and a lot of fun. At the time, he was a schoolteacher and I told him that he was a natural salesman and I referred him to one of my customers who hired him immediately. Ironically, a little over a year later I joined that same company as GM and we became coworkers.

Chris and Christina's biggest fear came true in the fall of 2015 when some lower stomach pain revealed cancer in her colon and a larger more intrusive mass on her liver. Chris was devastated and like any of us had many questions to ask God, like why her, why now? They had a three-year-old boy and an eight-month-old daughter. Why would God potentially take away a new mother? I don't blame Chris and would most likely ask the same questions if in the same situation. Christina, though, had a different mindset. Hers was one of full dependance and trust that Jesus would heal her; that He would show up and show off during all of the pain and suffering and bring ultimate peace.

Together they went on a journey to fight off this cancer which involved many highs and lows. They opted out of chemo due to the harshness of the treatments and the low percentage of success and quality of life that was told could follow. She began rounds of fusion treatments which showed immediate success out the gate as her numbers began to fall. There was hope, there was excitement, but fear would still creep in. I had the privilege of reading a handful of her journal entries recorded during this battle and even through the darkest moments, she proclaimed God's goodness. She didn't ask why her, but she bathed herself in scripture and the promises of God. When praying in December 2015, Christina heard God speak to her saying; "You will walk right through this, watch me split the sea for you. Do you trust me?" Wow!

She also wrote: "You are my anchor and my peace; you give me great joy in the midst of the storm."

And, probably the rawest and sweetest journal entry came on 2.8.2016 when she wrote:

"This is hard. Fear is scary. It gets so loud. I'm mad, I'm frustrated. I don't want to be here again. I want it gone for good. But it comes again and again and I'm finding it's You. Your voice is the only voice louder. Your word is the only truth truer. Your love is the only love that's perfect. The only love that completely casts out fear.

Draw me closer, put me nearer to you. Put your heart in me. Fill me with your love – then let me overflow and overflow into everyone around me. I love you."

What a prayer. What faith. What trust.

Unfortunately, Christina's battle took a turn for the worst a few months later and the doctors were no longer able to remove any more tumors or offer treatment. She went home on June 17th to be greeted by hospice. On the 20th she told Chris that she was "ready to be with Jesus, but not unless you say it's okay." His response was poignant and beautiful: "you have fought hard, and you have ran the race better than anyone I know. You've honored Jesus in such an incredible way. And yes, if you are ready to see Jesus... run to Him. He will make you well and you will be healed." Later that evening she called Chris over and said these words that have been spoken to so many people and continue to do so even today: "Chris, I'm going to die soon. And at the end of the day, it doesn't matter how long you live. But all that matters is truly knowing Jesus and putting your faith in Him. Chris, Run to Jesus, He's all that matters."

Christina passed away the next morning surrounded by family reading scripture and singing praises to Jesus. You may say: Well, God didn't hear her and heal her. He didn't part the seas. I would say that you are absolutely wrong. He healed her immediately upon her last breath and He parted the seas and led her right to the feet of Jesus. No more pain, no more suffering, cancer free. As I scroll through her Facebook page now almost seven years later, you still see the stories of hope and encouragement. Even recently, a stranger reached out to Chris and said that he read their story and it inspired her to go to church for the first time in many years.

So, you may ask, how does this story relate to raising kids? My response is, how does it not? There are so many underlying themes that will encompass the rest of this book. Themes like trusting Jesus no matter what, obedience vs understanding, not giving way to fear, perseverance, leaving a legacy, living a life of substance, that life is precious, journaling and on and on. Dadvoted reader, we only get one chance to raise our kids and point them in the right direction. They will follow our lead on how we react to all seasons of life, especially the tough ones. I leave you with the very words that Christina said as her last, "Run to Jesus, He's all that matters!"

OPPOSITE DAY

I **NEED YOU** to dig deep in the memory bank on this one. Do you remember as a child playing the game opposite day? You would speak, say or do the opposite of what you intended to speak, say or do. In fact, I just googled opposite day and low and behold I found out that January 25th is National Opposite Day! Very random, I know, and you are probably wondering where I am going with this, and I promise that I will bring this full circle.

The world we live in today says lots of things that are contrary to what the Bible says.

*The world says: Acquire as much as you can. The Word says: "It is better to give than to receive" Acts 20:35

*The world says: Live for yourself. The Word says: "put others before yourself." Phil 2:3-4

*The world says: Make as much money as you can. The Word says: "The love of money is the root of all evil." 1 Tim 6:10

*The world says: Fight those who oppose you. The Word says: "Love your enemies" Luke 6:27-29

***The world says:** Hold a grudge, do not forgive: **The Word says:** "Forgive as I have forgiven you" Esp 4:32

***The world says:** Sex before marriage is a must so you know what you are getting into. **The Word says:** "Keep the marriage bed pure" Heb 13:4

***The world says:** If it feels good do it. **The Word says:** "Too much of a good thing is a bad thing" Prov 25:16

***The world says:** You can choose your gender. **The Word says:** "So God created mankind in his own image, in the image of God he created them; male and female he created them." Gen 1:27

***The world says:** Abortion is OK. **The Word says:** "Do not put an innocent person to death" Exodus 23:7

***The world says:** Some sins are worse than others. **The Word says:** All sins are equal in God's eyes. 1 John 5:17

***The world says:** God will never forgive you for that: **The Word says:** "I have removed your transgressions as far as the east is from the west." Psalm 103: 11-12

***The world says:** Homosexual relationships are OK. **The Word says:** "Neither the sexually immoral nor idolaters nor adulterers nor men who have sex with men will inherit the kingdom of God." 1 Cor 6:9-11

Assuming you get my point here, the words of God are opposite to those of the world. The question is: Are we living more along the lines of God's word or the world? Or a little of both. That's a tough one to answer and absorb.

Look, I know some of these statements above are very controversial today and more so than ever before. I will not apologize for these words. Some will say that the Bible isn't relevant today. I say, it's more relevant and necessary than ever before.

Let's tackle how I approach the difficult conversations with my kids. Take sex before marriage as an example. When having this talk with Keaton, I told him biblically that we believe that sex is so powerful, and it's a great gift from God to married couples. I then said that not everyone believes this, nor do they follow this. This doesn't make them a bad person; it is what they believe just as we believe and base our life on what God's word says. I then say that we will never judge or condemn someone for what they believe, but always stay calm and act in love towards everyone.

Or let's review the very controversial topic of homosexuality. Let's read the whole verse first as I think we are very good at honing in on one fraction of a verse and not the whole verse.

"Or do you not know that wrongdoers will not inherit the kingdom of God? Do not be deceived: Neither the sexually immoral nor idolaters nor adulterers nor men who have sex with men nor thieves nor the greedy nor drunkards nor slanderers nor swindlers will inherit the king of God" (1 Cor 6:9-10).

So, it is very normal for us to look only at the homosexual portion of this and point a finger. When I go back and count, I find nine acts of wrongdoing in this passage. I'll be the first to admit, I have broken all of those except having sex with men. So, who am I to take that one sin listed and fully condemn someone as I am just as guilty or not more so due to the other eight issues that I have blatantly struggled with? Sidenote, don't assume I've committed adultery, but let me remind you of the second half of that verse when

47

Jesus says: "But I tell you that anyone who looks at a woman lustfully has already committed adultery with her in his heart" (Matt 5:28).

The main point here is that "all have sinned and fall short of the glory of God" (Rom 3:23). So where is our hope? Thankfully it comes in the very next verse: "And that is what some of you were. But you were washed, you were sanctified, you were justified in the name of the Lord Jesus Christ and by the Spirit of our God." 1 Cor 6:11 Praise God for that quick answer.

I know these are difficult topics to have conversations about. But you must be prepared. If you don't have a response in the moment, tell your kids that you will come back to them when you can better answer this tough question. And then come back and answer it! Don't brush it under the rug or hope they will forget. The biggest reminder is to always act in love and accept all people in whatever stage of life they are in. Remember **the Word says**: "We are in the world, but we are not of the world." John 17:16 And that we are "strangers in the world." 1 Peter 2:11

There are so many further verses about what we are up against as believers during this short tour on Earth:

> "Do not conform to the pattern of this world but be transformed by the renewing of your mind. Then you will be able to test and approve what God's will is – His good, pleasing and perfect will" (Rom 12:2).

> "Do not love the world or the things of the world. If anyone loves the world, the love of the Father is not in him. For all that is in the world – the desires of the flesh and the desires of the eyes and the pride in possessions – is not from the Father but is from the world. And the world is passing away along with its

desires, but whoever does the will of God abides forever" (1 John 2:15-17).

"You adulterous people, don't you know that friendship with the world means enmity against God? Therefore, anyone who chooses to be a friend of the world becomes and enemy of God" (James 4:4).

"Set your minds on things that are above, not on things that are on this earth" (Col 3:2).

Dadvoted reader, as believers, we celebrate Opposite Day every day and not just on January 25th! I hope this doesn't overwhelm you but empowers you to live your life all in for the Kingdom, knowing that people may ridicule you. But don't forget, they did that to Jesus as well.

ANXIETY

I CAN HONESTLY say that anxiety was never talked about growing up in the early 80's. We were taught to suppress any anxious feelings and to toughen up. I will agree that today, we really need to toughen up on a lot of topics and areas that I won't go into, but the anxiety front is something that I now believe is real and can't be ignored. Now just into my 40's, I never realized that this was happening all around me. In fact, many of my friends and a few family members have surfaced over the past year and admitted that they have struggled in some way with anxiety and have battled through it with or without help, support, or medication. I have coworkers that battle anxiety on many different levels. A lot of kids have anxious thoughts and feelings battling within their little minds. I'm no medical scholar, nor can I speak to the why behind it. Is it hereditary? Is it more prevalent today due to the pressures and stress of society? Is it based on certain shows or things our kids (or even maybe parents or teachers) are putting in their minds? Does lack of sleep, exercise or nutrition have anything to do with different levels of anxiety? What part does social media play?

All I can say, is that I don't know. Regarding my kids, I can also say that I have two kiddos, one with no signs of anxiety and one showing extreme moments of anxious thoughts. Both of my kids have been raised in the same household, both watch the same shows, both have the same parents and teachers and both eat very well and sleep like angels every night (once we get them there).

How do we attack anxiety? I first lean on scripture. Phil 4:6 says: "Do not be anxious about anything, but in every situation, by prayer and petition, with thanksgiving, present your requests to God." And the promise then follows quickly in verse 7 saying: "And the peace of God, which transcends all understanding, will guard your hearts and your minds in Christ Jesus."

Okay, this is a great place to start. This "book" written thousands of years ago seems very relevant today on the topic of anxiety. This also reiterates that this book is alive (Hebrews 4:12)! I do have some practical thoughts on dealing with anxious thoughts, but first I can't just skim over these words written in Philippians by Paul and want to unpack them a little more:

"Do not be anxious about <u>anything</u>" – It doesn't say some things or the big things? No, it says ANYTHING! Broken down in Greek that means, ANYTHING!

"But by prayer and petition" – We all know what prayer is, but petition in this sense is used as a verb that means humble appeal. This is deep rooted prayer and dependance on God to rescue you from this moment of anxiety, knowing that He is the true source of comfort and peace.

"With thanksgiving" – Praying through the situation with a heart and mindset that God is going to use this anxiousness for good. Somehow, someway, regardless of how dire the situation may be or feel at the time.

"Present your requests to God" – Tell Him what you are facing and what you need. Desperately seeking His hand of favor and removal of these anxious thoughts with the expectation that He is going to show up big.

And now the Promise in verse 7 shows up:

"And the peace of God" – Peace, one of the fruits of the spirit and only truly attained as a gift from God.

"Which transcends all understanding" – Meaning this probably won't make sense to the world. How could you walk through this without breaking is what they may say or be thinking?

"Will guard your hearts and your minds in Christ Jesus" – Your heart and mind will be protected. These thoughts will cease. You can breathe. You are not drowning.

So, you may be thinking, this is easy for me to sit behind a computer and tell you that you got this. That all you must do is open your bible and this will all go away. That I don't know what you are going through and how bad your situation is, and I agree. I don't know how bad your situation is. I don't know what your child is experiencing, or even you. I also would be remiss if I didn't discuss practical and tangible steps that are healthy to incorporate to work through anxious moments. Again, we've experienced and are currently working through this situation with one of our boys right now.

First, you must be sensitive to the situation. This, I think, was the hardest thing for me to accept because of my upbringing. I didn't really understand or want to admit that we had any sort of a problem. I also tend to be a fixer, so my next question was, how do we make this go away? A lot of his anxious moments came when he was going to be somewhere new where we weren't going to be with him, or even with events that we were used to attending, just taking place at a new location or with different kids, like swim meets. We learned that it was best to discuss these events in advance and to pray over my little guy. We would say "would mommy or daddy do anything to put you in harm's way?" Then we would ask him to pray to Jesus to calm his spirit and to protect him.

At night we still have anxious moments and setbacks based on fears and even some of the awful things third graders know and are talking about at school. So, every night we do what he calls his breathing. I have him lay still and I ask him to start at the tips of his toes and to relax them. And to slowly work his way up his legs and his fingers and his arms, through his chest and to the top of his head. During this time, I ask him to breath very slowly and calm his body. I sing to him, and it usually works. Now I know I may sound like super dad here, but trust me, after this if he comes back downstairs after five minutes in his room—I usually want to dropkick his butt across the room! Either way, it is a special moment, and it works most of the time.

Finally, we did get him into a Christian kid's counselor to work with him. She was highly recommended and very booked up, but once she heard our story, she began to work him into her rotation. I didn't attend these sessions and can't speak well to what she did, but I highly suggest consulting friends, as we did, to find a local source. I'm not going to speak to medication as I am no professional, by any means, but my opinion would be to do your research from multiple sources before taking this route.

All in, I pray that your kids don't battle with anxiety at any level or stage in life. My hope is that you root them in Phil 4:6-7 and you do it for yourself as well. I will admit, that even after writing the first part of this entry, I had an extremely tough day and battled many anxious thoughts. I laughed most of them off as an attack from the enemy but still had to pray through. Thankfully, God showed up during my commute that morning and when I turned on the radio, the same song I sing my little guy each night was the first song that came on the radio as I was getting on the highway. *Thank you, Lord, that you've got us and you capture and control our anxiousness.*

Song Lyrics: "Lord, I need you, oh, I need you. Every hour I need You. My one defense, my righteousness. Oh God, how I need You" (Matt Maher).

GOD <u>WILL</u> GIVE YOU MORE THAN YOU CAN HANDLE

SAY WHAT? YOU have probably all heard and possibly said this line before: "God won't give you more than you can handle." This is by far one of the most misquoted statements and, by the way, is not in the Bible. I understand that this may be said to give someone comfort during a tough season or moment in life. I get it. Or, it might be said to help someone pick themselves up and to persevere through a battle they are in. But if you really think about it, I believe that God <u>will</u> give you more than you can handle so that your dependence on Him will increase. Or maybe He will allow you to go through a tough situation so that you call upon Him and have Him shape you through it. I know for a fact that I couldn't handle losing a child or an unexpected sickness that would only give Keeli months to live. I pray I don't experience any of those things, but I know I have a firm foundation to lean on if life threw me a curveball.

Probably the hardest verse in the Bible for me to obey is James 1:2-4: "Consider it pure joy, my brothers and sisters, whenever you face trails of many kinds, because you know that the testing of your faith produces perseverance. Let perseverance finish its work so that you may be mature and complete, not lacking anything." Below is a journal entry I made in Keaton's Bible that I plan to give him when he graduates high school:

"Keaton, this is one of the hardest passages for me to obey. "Consider it pure joy when you face trials." This is crazy talk. We hate problems. When problems arise, we are quick to complain or say "why me," or go into hiding. But the Bible says otherwise. "Because this testing produces perseverance which will make you mature and complete, not lacking anything." Wow! What a promise. I want to be mature and complete, and I want that for you. So, face trials head on knowing that this promise from God will be revealed."

You may be thinking, well, this isn't fair. The God of the universe, who loves me would allow me to go through trials and tough seasons. And the answer is yes. One day we can look Jesus in the face and ask the why questions, which I have plenty of them, some deep and others not so deep (like why mosquitos and what's the purpose of roaches), but that's neither here nor there. There are many references to trials faced in the Bible by key characters, but there are three that stick out to me.

Job – Job was considered by God as "blameless and upright, a man who fears God and shuns evil" (Job 1:8). God allowed Job to suffer tremendously physical painful ailments, his entire wealth and livelihood were taken away in an instant and he had ten kids of his die. Definitely more than he could handle, and I think I would curl up in a ball and be done. Job was clearly shaken and thought, as many of us would, that all of this traced back to a sin he had committed, which it didn't. God allowed him to go through this to prove to Satan that there were still big lovers of God out there full of faith that existed no matter what the circumstance. Again, this is a tough story to absorb, but God did redeem it, healed Job, restored his possessions, and blessed him with 10 more children. Job's faith rings loudly when he said, "I know that my Redeemer lives, and that in the end he will stand upon the earth" (Job 19:25).

Paul – Paul went through so many trials and persecution. In his prior life, he was known as Saul who persecuted and murdered Christians before Jesus rescued and renamed him Paul, where he became the greatest advocate for Christ and wrote most of the New Testament. His list of trials and suffering as a believer are detailed in 2 Cor 11:23-28: "I have worked much harder, been in prison more frequently, been flogged more severely, and been exposed to death again and again. Five times I received from the Jews the forty lashes minus one. Three times I was beaten with rods, once I was pelted with stones, three times I was shipwrecked, I spent a night and a day in the open sea. I have been constantly on the move. I have been in danger from bandits, in danger from my fellow Jews, in danger from Gentiles; in danger in the city, in danger in the country, in danger at sea; and in danger from false believers. I have labored and toiled and have often gone without sleep; I have known hunger and thirst and have often gone without food; I have been cold and naked. Besides everything else, I face daily the pressure of my concern for all the churches."

God clearly gave Paul more than he could handle. And I think he so pointedly shows where he drew his strength from when he said: "For to me, to live is Christ and to die is gain" (Phil 1:21).
Jesus – Jesus came to earth for two main purposes: to serve and save. The mere fact that God would humble Himself to come to earth in the form of a baby, yes, a baby that needed his diaper changed and bottle fed to Him is still hard to fathom. Moreover, that he would die a gruesome death via crucifixion and bare the weight of the world's past, present and future sins was almost too much for Him to handle. He actually cries out and pleads for God to take this away from him in Mathew 25:39. In Mathew 25:38 Jesus said, "My soul is overwhelmed with sorrow to the point of death." So even here

you see that God allowed even Jesus to be overwhelmed with more than He could handle. We also know the end of the story. That Jesus died but defeated hell, death and the grave when he was raised to life 3 days later paying the ultimate sacrifice and giving all who believe and call on the name of Jesus eternal life.

All three of these are very extreme and intense situations that probably don't give you the warm and fuzzies. In fact, I'm nervous writing on this topic in hopes that I'm not challenged myself with what I am writing about (which seems to happen often). We can't walk in fear or tiptoe around. We just have to be prepared by being bathed in scripture.

This might be deep stuff to speak to your children about when they are young. In fact, I just talked briefly about this with Keaton tonight. At eleven, he's a deep thinker and an old soul. I told him about this misused saying and he kind of shrugged and went on about his evening. This was maybe bad timing on my part, but I know there will be many more instances where I will need to speak truth to him and to instill that there may be moments in life that God will give him more than he can handle and for him to lean on Jesus more and to fully depend on Him. The worst thing I could ever tell my boys is that once they trust Jesus that there will be no more problems. We live in a fallen, broken world. Some might say you will face more problems as a believer. I'm not going to debate that here, but I am going to live out these tough moments with my eyes, heart, soul and mind on Jesus the true comforter, knowing and believing in his promises, especially the three below:

"Consider it pure joy, my brothers and sisters, whenever you face trails of many kinds, because you know that the testing of your faith produces perseverance. Let perseverance finish its work so that you may be mature and complete, not lacking anything" (James 1:2-4).

"I have told you these things so that in me you
may have peace. In this world, you will have
trouble. But take heart! I have overcome the world"
(John 16:33).

"God works ALL things for good for those who
love Him and are called according to His purpose"
(Rom 8:28).

Dadvoted reader, God will give you more than you can handle.
That's okay. You aren't alone. He's drawing you and leading you to
a greater thing. He is preparing you, making you complete so that
you won't be lacking anything. If you accept this (though it sucks),
God will redeem it and use it for good, somehow someway.

ONE LIFE

BEN FRANKLIN HAS been tagged with this famous quote from 1789: "In this world nothing can be said to be certain, except death and taxes." I won't speak to the latter part of this quote but will reiterate the first part: <u>death is unavoidable</u>. The good news is that if you put your hope, faith, and trust in Jesus, you receive the gift of eternal life. Thank you, Jesus! Many may think that eternal life happens when you die and meet Jesus in heaven. I would disagree with that thought. I believe that eternal life begins when you put your hope, faith, and trust in Jesus on earth. As a believer, you are called to align your thoughts and actions of heaven while still on this earth. You can walk with a full sense of peace and direction, knowing that your salvation is secure. You aren't perfect, but you recognize your sin and your short comings, and you turn from them. You live your life with purpose, and you pursue the things of God. You discover what God put you here on earth to accomplish for the Kingdom. Of course, not all of this is immediate and is a process. But my challenge, and I can say due to personal experience, is that life is short and we can't waste a second.

I had the opportunity just recently to speak in front of three classes of seniors in the Industrial Distribution program at Texas A&M University. This came about through my good friend and mentor Bob, who is a professor on staff. It was a great experience and was very fruitful to sit in front of some very talented and bright kids. One of the biggest points I said to them was that I wished I had kept up a hunger for learning immediately after college and into my 30s. Now at 40, continual learning is vital to my growing, changing and adding value to the folks I lead at home and in the workplace. I also talked to them about finding their passion and that my newfound passion, other than being with my family, was centered around writing and coaching people.

After my first session, I had a gentleman named Seth walk up to me to pick my brain about the multi-family industry in hopes that I could connect him with apartment owners to walk with him in his early journey. I could immediately tell by his demeanor that Seth was different. He was calm and collected, very mature for his age, and I could see peace in his eyes. He was wearing a bracelet that said "pray hard" on it and it clicked. This guy loves Jesus. My original thought was, "do people see this in me upon their first interaction?" That's a challenging one to ask and I will continue to ask myself that same question. That afternoon we texted back and forth, and I mentioned that I could see he had a strong faith and I told him to keep pressing in and running after Jesus. He responded back with "Yes sir! Jesus is my MAIN mission." This kid gets it! I want to meet his parents, I want to know his journey, I want my boys to tackle life with this mantra and mindset.

Instilling early that your kids only have one short life on Earth is so crucial. Life is short. Life is precious. Are they going to live to please themselves and, even worse, others, or are they going to live to please Jesus? I ask myself this same question, especially as one that struggles in the people-pleasing arena. Galatians 1:10 says: "Am I now trying to win the approval of human beings, or of God? Or am I trying to please people? If I were still trying to please people, I would not be a servant of Christ." 1 Thes: 2-4 says: "On the contrary, we speak as those approved by God to be entrusted with the gospel. We are not trying to please people but God, who tests our hearts."

I also don't want my boys to think they are too young to do something bold in life or for the Kingdom. Seth definitely doesn't believe this lie. That's why I pray 1 Timothy 4:12 over my boys: "Don't let anyone look down on you because you are young, but set an example for the believers in speech, in conduct, in love, in faith and in purity."

I've been on a major journey over the past 18 years since college. I have really no regrets (other than I wish I would have continued learning Spanish), but I still have time. Though I can honestly say, I've had way too many mediocre days where I lived for myself or with no direction. Thankfully, the Lord has stayed by my side through all of it and continued to mold and shape me. To the Dadvoted reader reading this, THE CLOCK IS TICKING! We must live a life of purpose and substance so we can show our kids the fruit of a life that is lived with purpose and substance. We must play a part in passing this down to them. Gary DeSalvo, my pastor growing up, who is now dancing with Jesus in Heaven, used to always remind us that one day we would have a headstone that would have our date of birth, a dash, followed by our date of death and then some verbiage under it summarizing our life. His saying was, "it's all about the dash." The dash (-) though one small character in size, means everything. The dash represents what we did on this short time on earth with the one life we were given. Life is a mist (James 4:14). We are here today and gone tomorrow. Don't miss out! Have no regrets!

FEARING GOD

I'M PRETTY SURE when my parents were growing up in the 60's, there was an unhealthy fear of God instilled in them and in that generation. Hell, fire and brimstone were thrown at church attenders from the pulpit as a way to scare people into salvation. Look, I'll even admit, I was officially "saved" at an event called Heaven's gates, Hell's flames in high school in the late 90s. This was a production that basically scared young kids into thinking about eternity by showing how gruesome and excruciating hell was. I'm not sure how Temple High School got this approved to take place on campus, but many attended and were "saved." Even though I had a love for Jesus in my heart, I felt that I had to seal it publicly. Scaring people into believing can work but doesn't mean that it will stick. Raising your hand and saying a public prayer so that you can sign off on your Fire Insurance policy isn't completely off, but it's not the point. It must be from the heart. It is the beginning of a journey, not a one-time event. Jesus wants us to have a relationship with Him. What does that really mean? Think about your closest friend. How do you interact? They know everything about you. You are in constant communication with each other. There is true love and respect for each other.

The Bible references fearing God numerous times:

Prov 1:7 "The fear of the Lord is the beginning of knowledge"

Psalm 34: 9-10 "Fear the Lord, you his holy people, for those who fear him lack nothing. The lions may grow weak and hungry, but those who seek the Lord lack no good thing."

Psalm 33: 8 "Let all the earth fear the Lord; let all the people of the world revere him."

But what does it really mean to fear God? For this, I'll lean on 2 sources that can explain it better than I can. Jeff Wells, lead pastor at WoodsEdge Community Church (my home church), and Tony Evans, pastor at Oak Cliff Bible Fellowship and also a nationally known speaker, writer and President of the Urban Alternative (on a sidenote, I also played football with his son Jonathan in college).

Jeff Wells states: "To fear God is to revere God. The idea is reverence, respect, awe. This is a reverential fear, not a cringing fear. This is a healthy and holy fear that obeys God because he is God and he is to be obeyed. It is our solemn duty and our glad privilege to obey the Lord."

Tony Evans states it in an even easier way to understand: "Fearing God means to take Him seriously. To fear God merges two concepts. One involves being afraid of something, and the other is being in awe of it. Fearing God isn't one or the other. It's a convergence of both. When you mix these two together – being afraid and in awe – it translates into a life that takes God seriously" (Evans, 2021).[5]

These two thoughts about fearing God really make me think. Do I really fear God? For me, I think as I have grown up and matured and traveled to many beautiful parts of the world, I have developed a deep awe and respect for the Lord. Just recently when I was in South Lake Tahoe, 9000 ft up in the mountains, looking over the deepest Lake in the US and its vast colors of blue, I was in awe of God and His creation. Even Rolando, my brother-in-law, stated when we were on the boat heading to Emerald Bay, "man, God really showed off here."

But the challenge for me comes in the other parts of these quotes. When Jeff says, "have a fear that obeys God because He is God" and when Tony says, "you must equally be in awe and afraid," I'm not sure I've fully feared the Lord or even feared Him many times. I think back to any time the presence of the Lord appeared in the Bible. They fell to their knees, they couldn't look, they couldn't speak. I haven't had these encounters but imagine I would do the same. The root point is, do I live in obedience to God? Do I take Him seriously, all the time? This isn't about following a set of rigid rules, checking off the church attendance box, giving a little money here and there, going to prayer service, and worshipping with my hands lifted high on Sunday (not that these are bad things). But am I fully surrendered to the Lordship of Jesus and obedient to ALL of his words all the time, even the hard ones, in ALL parts of my life? Even on the topics or verses I don't understand. Or even when I see all the bad in the world around us. Jeff Wells also has stated numerous times throughout the years, "understanding can wait, obedience cannot." One day, all these things will be revealed to us. But today we must live by faith and obedience.

Dadvoted reader, my challenge to you and to me is that we continually seek God, be obedient to His word and to take Him seriously. That we wouldn't walk in fear that the Lord is going to strike us down at any moment, but that we are in awe of Him. When we speak of Him to our kids that they see our tone change, that our eyes light up about the great God of the universe. That we strive to live a life that includes God in all aspects, and in everything we do, every decision we make and everything that we face. It's never too late to begin discussing a healthy fear of God. That God is our father and that just as we are called to obey our earthly Father, how even much more should be obey our Heavenly Father who made us in His image. Our kids need to know this. It is our responsibility to teach and live it out so that it sticks.

THE BATTLE

I MUST ADMIT that this topic is unsettling. It is also something not talked about as often as it should be in church and around most believers. We frequently talk about how Jesus saves, and He wants the best for us and wants us to follow Him. We talk about being new creations in Christ and striving for righteousness, which are all great and vital things. But I don't think we really understand what is going on behind the scenes. I was recently challenged by a coworker to dive in and learn more about the spiritual battle to understand and be more aware. Through this, I learned where the battle is attacking me, which has empowered me to surrender some things to Jesus. I now know that I can't win against the enemy by myself. He is too powerful, cunning, and persistent. The enemy gets off on our nonchalant attitude about the battle at hand and even more so, loves when we ignore it altogether. My goal is that we would become more "chalant"!

All jokes aside, the spiritual battle is very real, and we need to understand it more so we can go on the attack for our lives, our families and our kids. Every negative thing that is happening in our life is attached to the battle. EVERYTHING! That coworker that is slandering you at work, that family member that has gone astray and is living a destructive lifestyle, that addiction that keeps rearing its head, that inappropriate thought or lustful vision are all part of the battle. The people against you really aren't even the people against you, but a spiritual attack is on them that is flowing to you. Knowing this has helped me tremendously. I battle against a lot of folks in my career and now knowing that the enemy is playing a part through them against me gives me a lot more clarity and grace towards those hateful or challenging moments.

The Bible is very clear about the battle. Ephesians 6:12 says, "For our struggle is not against flesh and blood, but against the rulers, against the authorities, against the powers of this dark world and against the spiritual forces of evil in the heavenly realms." I've read over this verse so many times and tend to pass over it. Maybe because I don't want to understand this tough concept or because my puny brain can't absorb this. Also, the church doesn't speak on this often, perhaps due to lack of popularity as this isn't a "feel good" message, hence why this is unsettling to me and many of us. The enemy has assigned his minions over us to speak deceiving thoughts. Thoughts like, "do you think God is really good" or, "this is who you are, you will never be loved by God," or even justifiable thoughts like, "well, you know God is going to forgive you, so you might as well do it and just ask for forgiveness." The enemy is subtle. He's not on a megaphone, but issues soft nudges and whispers. The flipside to this is that God has assigned His angels over your life, who are here to protect you, and who are constantly praying over you and won't let the enemy get his claws fully into you. Psalm 91:11 says, "For He will command his angels concerning you to guard you in all your ways." We don't worship these angels, as we only worship God, but this should be comforting.

I think back to the story my friend Joy told us years ago when she grew up a missionary in Uganda which she retells here:

"My parents were missionaries in Uganda, Africa and we lived there for 13 years. There were four other families there as well that we were very close to. It was the time when Idi Amin was president and there were a lot of armed thugs, soldiers looting, and rebel war-riors killing missionaries. The times we unsafe. But our families kept doing what we were called to do; meeting and starting groups, sus-taining churches, training pastors, and visiting villages. One night one of our families and their six young children heard lots of noise and gunshots all around them. At bedtime, Harry and Dorris, the parents, were making their rounds singing and praying to help ease the kids who were scared and crying. Then from one side of the house a kid yelled, "Dad!!! It's so bright!" They looked out and saw a huge guy with wings flapping right outside the window. Then from the other side of the house, another kid started yelling, "Mom! Dad! Quick come here! I see angels, they're so bright!!" Later they heard from others in the village that the warriors and looters had seen angels surrounding a house they were trying to invade and were ter-rified and ran. We all knew that God had covered them in His love and protection and that it was a powerful experience."

What a radical story of God's power and protection for His people. I fully believe that He is surrounding believers today even though most of us aren't facing extreme danger.

Let's get back to the unseen battle. How do we handle the spir-itual battle that is raging all around us in heavenly realms? How about we attack it head on. For starters, we pray against it, but we also pray for awareness. 1 Peter 5:8 says "Be alert and of sober mind. Your enemy the devil prowls around like a roaring lion looking for someone to devour." But be aware, when you pray for awareness, most likely you are going to become aware of something quickly.

A few months ago, I prayed; "Lord help me to be aware of the spiritual battle today." Later at work I was faced with a frustrating situation where my team hid something from me that came to head and was going to cost the company $19,000. I was furious to say the least knowing that this could have been avoided if we hadn't sat on it and communicated better. I dove in to try and put all the puzzle pieces together beginning by pulling the PO. It was "HOU666." Seriously? I sat back and said, "Ok devil, I see you trying to get under my skin today." Thankfully I laughed this off and went back to the grind. I didn't stew in it, apologized to the folks I got a little crazy with, and vowed to use this as a teaching moment. This was a mild attack in nature, or maybe felt mild as I was prepared for it in advance. What's attacking you today? Who or what does the enemy have against you that is causing you to retreat from the things of God or causing you to act in such a way that is not of God? These are tough questions, but I challenge you to ponder and ask God to reveal what is against you right now.

To my Dadvoted reader, we cannot avoid the battle any longer! The enemy is a deceiver and is out to ruin your life, your marriage, and your kid's futures. We must gear up! We must go on the attack! We have too much at stake. How do we protect ourselves, or families and our children? We put on the full armor of God.

THE ARMOR OF GOD

PRIOR TO VERSE 12 in Ephesians 6, Paul says in verse 11; "Put on the full armor of God, so that you can take your stand against the devil's schemes." The then in verse 13 reiterates it when he says, "Therefore put on the full armor of God, so that when the day of evil comes, you may be able to stand your ground, and after you have done everything, to stand."

> "Stand firm then, with the **belt of truth**, buckled around your waste, with the **breastplate of righteousness** in place, and with your feet fitted with the readiness that comes from the **gospel of peace**, and in addition to all of this, take up the **shield of faith**, with which you can extinguish all the flaming arrows of the evil one. Take the **helmet of salvation** and the **sword of the Spirit**, which is the word of God." Eps 6: 14-17

This is how a Dadvoted warrior gears up for battle! We are prepared, we are equipped with truth, we are protected with righteousness and faith, secure in our salvation, and we have the word of God as our weapon. With this, the enemy can't penetrate us or our families!

Finally, here is the best news of all. We know the end of the story! We know who wins in the end and we are on the winning side! We aren't sitting idle watching a rivalry football game on the edge of our seats, hoping that we win. We know the ending. That Jesus is coming back for His people and that He will defeat the enemy once and for all. This doesn't mean that there won't be some ups and downs along the way. That there won't be some turnovers or injuries that hit us dead in the face. But we stand with confidence! We are aware of the enemy, but not afraid of the enemy. God has him on a leash and he won't prevail. Stand firm!

GRATITUDE AND CONTENTMENT

THE COMMON PHRASE "an attitude of gratitude," has a great ring to it. As a marketing guru, I love anything that flows together via rhyming, alliteration, or combined words, hence Dadvoted. This creates a higher opportunity for stickiness, meaning it will be more memorable. That's every marketer's dream. For example, If I sing to you in jingle format, "give me a break, give me a break," you're most likely going to respond back with, "break me off a piece of that Kit-Kat bar." Or, if I say "milk", your response might be: "it does a body good." Marketing and stickiness are far from the topics I want to expand on today, so back to gratitude. Gratitude, which lies deep in your heart, determines your outlook on life. Most of us are very grateful overall for the big things. Those things that are easy to see and are almost a given. We live in the greatest country in the world and don't have to worry about things like fresh water, clean air, electricity and so on. I consider myself pretty tough and resilient but take electricity away from me for more than an hour or so and I'm a complete mess. Not only will I start to fret about keeping food cold, but I will also attempt to flip light switches and use the microwave as I am conditioned to the simplicities of life. We live in a society of ease and comfort. I'm not going to say that this is a bad thing, but do want to press your thinking a little bit today. The world around us says that contentment comes from the accumulation of things, money, accomplishments, and status. That if we have the latest and greatest and the most, that we will be happy and content. Jim Carey is known for saying, "I think everybody should get rich and famous and do everything they ever dreamed of so they can see it's not the answer." This is pretty shocking, as most would not think of these words coming from him or let alone any celebrity. I'm not sure if Carey has a foundation of faith, or has just lived this firsthand, but appears that his worldly significance and accomplishments haven't guaranteed complete fulfillment in life as he might have thought prior to his celebrity status.

Gratitude and contentment are intertwined. If you have a deep-felt gratitude in life, your level of contentment will mirror the gratitude you possess. The Bible speaks to contentment in such a sobering way. In 1 Timothy 6: 6-8 the Bible says, "But godliness with contentment is great gain. For we brought nothing into the world, and we can take nothing out of it. But if we have food and clothing, we will be content with that." Simply put, food and clothing are all we need.

Phil 4:12 Paul also says, "I know what it is to be in need, and I know what it is to have plenty. I have learned the secret of being content in any and every situation, whether well fed or hungry, whether living in plenty or in want." Think back to biblical times; they didn't have running water, electricity, grocery stores or Uber Eats at a click of a button. Heaven forbid, there was no Amazon. My protein powder that I ordered yesterday on Amazon... wait for it... showed up yesterday. Yet, I still get so worked up when a grocery store closes on a holiday to give their employees rest. Or, when the gas pump is working a little slower than it should. I struggle with being content in all circumstances but am real good at being content when everything is going my way. I also must remember that Paul is writing this while sitting in prison!

True gratitude stems from knowing the Giver. James 1:17 says, "Every good and perfect gift is from above, coming down from the

Father of heavenly lights, who does not change like shifting shadows." Every good thing we have is from God. Every feeling, every good meal, every experience, every victory, everything, including your kids. Dadvoted man, where is your hope found? Where do you draw your joy from, your peace from, your contentment from, your gratitude from? My hope that it is from the Father, the ultimate giver, and not from the world. I'm not saying that working hard and accomplishing victories is a bad thing. In fact, we are called and made for that, but where is your heart and what's its deep desire? Our hearts are tied to our minds which are directly tied to our actions and words. Are we consumed with status and accumulating more? If so, our kids will see this, and it will rub off on them. They will want more and expect contentment to follow. Do our kids know that every good and perfect gift is from above? Are we telling them that? Do they know how good we have it? I'm not just speaking to the super successful here, but to majority of every American dad that will read these words in this book. Let me help put it in more perspective with the quote below:

"If you have food in your fridge, clothes on your back, a roof over your head and a place to sleep you are richer than 75% of the world. If you have money in the bank, your wallet, and some spare change, you are among the top 8% of the world's wealthy. If you work up this morning with more health than illness you are more blessed than the million people who will not survive this week. If you have never experienced the danger of battle, the agony of imprisonment or torture, or the horrible pangs of starvation you are luckier than 500 million people alive and suffering. If you can read this message you are more fortunate than 3 billion people in the world who cannot read it at all" (Unknown).

This quote puts a lot of things in perspective for me as both a man and as a father. I'm grateful for the journey I'm on for raising my boys to become great men of God and I hope you are as well. How do we stay the course or get back on track? Hebrews 12:1-2 says, "Let us throw off everything that hinders and the sin that so easily entangles. And let us run with perseverance the race marked out for us, <u>fixing our eyes on Jesus</u>, the pioneer and perfecter of faith." It's not too late. If you have been stuck in finding gratitude and contentment in "things" that are meaningless, change today. Seek the Lord and ask Him to change your heart. Then make tangible changes and have conversations with your kids and tell them that you are pivoting to what you thought was meaningful to now what God says is meaningful and you will change.

GIVING

I DON'T THINK I am out of line when I say that we naturally instill receiving in our kids right out the gate versus a heart of giving. Christmas, birthdays, and other holidays are times when we as parents, and especially grandparents, shower our kids and grandkids with gifts to celebrate them. These are sweet and documented moments that flood our photo albums and our memories for years and years. It is precious to see our kids get something that they really wanted, or to surprise them with something they never thought they would get. There is no doubt that I will never forget my boys' reactions when we adopted our dog Zoey and she became our first real pet (I don't count the beta fish we had prior, though we kept one alive for over 2 years!). But how do we begin to transition into teaching our kids that it is better to give than to receive (Acts 20:3)? At what point will the light switch turn on and they will see and feel the goodness and warmth that giving provides? We are by no means there yet, but I'm seeing hope as we start to subtly emphasize that it's not all about them. They enjoy creating gifts for friends and family members and going shopping for Keeli for Christmas and Mother's Day. Unfortunately, I am instilling the last second, day before mentality into them as well, which I admit, I need to work on. But regardless, giving is so much more than just giving gifts to the people we know, love and cherish. There are so many other ways to give that is more meaningful. A handful that come to mind include, giving our time, giving encouragement, giving to those in need and giving back to Jesus (that's right, I'm going there). Let me explain these a little further:

Giving time – What first comes to mind here is that of serving. There are so many opportunities to serve in the church and in your community. Some of the most rewarding time serving for Keeli and I were during the years we did high school ministry. I will admit, I usually entered most high school bible study groups extremely whooped from the day but left many of them extremely rejuvenated. My boys at a young age would also sit with my group at times, if the topic was appropriate for their little ears. This gave them an opportunity to see us serve and my hope was that it would rub off on them as they got older. Today, Keaton is already helping in the younger kids' ministry with puppets and tech, so it appears to be doing just that. I think the main point is that your kids begin to understand that it's not all about them. That there are ways to get outside of yourself and help others. And what stems from that can be very rewarding and challenge you to become better overall. It's best to uncover what you are passionate about vs. just serving for serving sake. There are so many uses for your talents. Only special people are called to change other people's kid's diapers in the nursery (I'm not one of them). But I've been called to lead and speak. What's your talent that can be used to serve others or the church? There are numerous possibilities. Don't be a spectator, get in the game!

Giving encouragement – Probably the hardest thing about giving encouragement is remembering to give encouragement. It means you must be fully aware. We get so overwhelmed and busy, that we can forget to really look for these opportunities to encourage and brighten folk's days. But there are opportunities all around us. Seek the Lord to soften your heart to those around you and open your eyes. Just this morning, I asked the Lord to provide me someone I needed to check in on and encourage and the name Josh just came to mind right before I started writing. On my commute in today, Josh, who I haven't talked to in 6 months will get a call. The world is so negative, especially right now. We must be big encouragers to not only our kids, but to those all around us.

I have a gal that I work with named Gabby. She comes in daily, is quiet and reserved and does her job. It's easy for her to get lost in the shuffle. Last year, she walked into my office to give me something to sign off on and I stopped her and told her that I appreciate how consistent she is, how she never misses work or calls in sick and that I appreciated her. Her eyes lit up and she looked at me and said, "thank you so much for telling me that. I really am glad that you see that in me." Let me remind you, that I'm no saint, and I fall short <u>A LOT</u>. But this was so easy. I had noticed this about Gabby for months, but never stopped to tell her that she was special and was standing out in the group. My challenge for all of us is to find the good in people and bring it out. Especially in our kids. Encourage them! It is contagious!

<u>Giving to those in need</u> – I would love to sit here and tell you that I take my kids every Saturday to the homeless shelter to serve the needy. Now that I say that, I really need to start doing this to open their eyes. But we don't. Our Saturdays are full of activities ranging in birthday parties, swim meets, plays and performances, basketball games, housework, etc. We have started looping the boys in on ways we can help those in need. We participate in the giving tree every year at Christmas, where we sponsor a couple of kids who won't get Christmas gifts without the help from others. We chose kids around the same age as my boys and allow them to pick out a gift for them and we use it as a learning moment to tell them that not everyone is as fortunate as us. We also for the past few years have partnered with World Vision to send livestock for families to use in third world countries. Again, we use this as a family moment to decide (and maybe argue) over what animals will be the best for this family. These are small drops in the bucket, but my hope is that they are starting to mold our boys to understand that not everyone has it as good as we do.

As I mentioned above on seeking the Lord on encouraging moments, I would also nudge you to do the same when it comes to giving to those in need. About ten years ago, I went to Kroger to pick up some groceries. I was in there for probably twenty minutes, basically on a mission to get what I needed and to get out. After checking out and walking to my car, my heart was challenged by the Spirit. I thought to myself, man I didn't look one person in the eye, I didn't acknowledge anyone, not even the cashier. In that moment I prayed, "Father forgive me." If there is something that I missed, someone that needed my help, would you reveal that to me right now. Crazy prayer, right? Within seconds of that prayer, a truck pulled up to me and a gal rolled down her window. She was frantic and said that she was in trouble, that someone she knew had been abusive to her and she was fleeing and had nothing but what she was wearing. I saw the fear in her eyes. She said is there anything you can do to help me? In that moment, I didn't challenge it, I reached in my wallet and gave all the cash I had in it, which I think was around $60. The amount wasn't the point, I was going to give all of it. I don't find this story to be a coincidence, but Jesus showing up in that moment. Let's seek to help the needy. Don't focus on their past or any perceived motives, but on the heart of Jesus.

Giving back to Jesus – I know people squirm when tithing is brought up in church. And as I've experienced before, it's usually that one Sunday when you invite someone to church for the first time (insert eye roll emoji). But this is a safe place. You can skim over this, and move on, or muscle up and consider this obedient act. I'm not going to get too technical here on the rules and regulations of giving. Is it really ten percent? Is it pre-tax or post tax? Do I give back on the money I get back from my tax return? I'll let a bible scholar tackle those parts through your own research if you think that's relevant. I will say that it's about the heart and not about the head. 2 Cor 9:7 says, "Each one of you should give what you have decided in your heart to give, not reluctantly or under compulsion, for God loves a cheerful giver." I remember being extremely financially strapped when Keeli and I were first married in California, house poor, with only one income, and with one baby in the barn and another in the oven. I was stressed to the max. When reaching out to my brother-in-law Michael for his thoughts on giving, he reiterated this verse to me and challenged me to give out of love and not out of grudging obligation. Now could there have been some things I took out of my life at that time, probably, but at that time I was financially suffocating in that season we were in.

I tell you that story because I know those stories are real. I also recall the woman giving out of her poverty and Jesus claiming that she had given more than the rich (Mark 12: 41-44). I do believe that giving back to God is a mindset shift. First of all, it's not your money anyway. It's from God. Second, it's about obedience and not obligation. It's a litmus test of your faith. Do you trust God enough to give him your first fruits and not your leftovers? Proverbs 3: 9-10 says it the best: "Honor the Lord with your wealth, with the first fruits of all your crops: then your barns will be filled to overflowing, and your vats will brim over with new wine." Third, I believe that God is truly using my financial gifts to further the Kingdom and doing things with it that I may never know until I am on the other side of this earth in Heaven. I am thankful to attend WoodsEdge Church in The Woodlands, TX, that is debt free and gives over half of the income outside the walls to further the Kingdom. They don't promote this much from the pulpit, but our giving is doing major things throughout the world to help point people to Jesus. But they are also doing lots of little things to help those struggling in our area and around Houston. I've heard stories of single moms receiving a car to help them get to work and of families in need being blessed with housing. Again, this isn't promoted, so I can't really give you all the stories, but I can tell you my heart and prayer when I click send on my monthly tithe to the church. I pray that God will use His money that I'm giving back to His church to bless someone and point them to Jesus. And that one day I will meet that person face to face in Heaven and they will tell me what my offering did to change their life and the lives of the people around them, because it pointed them to Jesus. There is also a promise that comes with the verse above that says, "your barns will be filled to overflowing." I'm not going to dissect this part either or provide you false hope, but I believe that God will bless the cheerful giver in many ways in His timing. I'm going to continue to trust and be obedient. I pray that you will journey with me on giving, because I really don't think you can teach your kids this, unless you are actively involved.

YOLO

I'LL ADMIT THAT I'm not the hippest anymore when it comes to today's sayings and acronyms. I usually have to be brought up to speed by one of the younger sales reps on my team, the high school kids from church, or even more shameful utilizing Google or Alexa to help keep me in the know. Merriam-Webster even adopted the following new acronyms in late 2021 as part of their new words for the year including: FWIW "for what it's worth", ICYMI "in case you missed it", TBH "to be honest", and FTW "for the win". So, ICYMI and FWIW and TBH, I wanted to write about YOLO, FTW of course. Say what?

I can honestly say (TBH), that I've known the acronym YOLO for many years, though never used it. That changes today! So, to keep you from asking Alexa, YOLO or "you only live once," first dated back to the Frank Sinatra Film in 1937, "You only live once," though the acronym was claimed to be tagged by Grateful Dead drummer Mickey Hart, when purchasing and renaming his Sonoma, CA Ranch "Yolo" in 1996. The saying actually picked up popularity in the late 2000's. Either way, I really don't need to pinpoint it's coming to existence or if people now think it is overused and needs to become extinct. But there is truth to this saying. You really do only live once. Shocker, right? This can be lived out and used or abused in one of two ways. 1. You live in the moment, often recklessly, to experience as much as you want to experience in the name of self-indulgence. 2. You live each day to its fullest knowing that life is short and you are placed here to make an impact in some way, form, or fashion. As, I've grown up and matured, which is still a work in progress, I lived in reason #1 for way too long but now am currently thriving in YOLO reason #2.

My source for YOLO reason #2 stems from the exact same acronym but tweaked just slightly. My YOLO version #2 stems from a spiritual YOLO now meaning "you only live for **One**." Jesus is the one where my life is centered, which changes everything! No longer am I only focused on myself and what makes me happy or feel good. Nor am I just laser focused on my children. I try my best to see the world and the people around me through the eyes of Christ. You may ask, how is that possible? The bible says in Gal 2:20, "I have been crucified with Christ and I no longer live, but Christ lives in me. The life I now live in the body, I live by faith in the Son of God, who loved me and gave Himself for me." I also believe that I was "bought with a price" and that I will "honor God with my body" (1 Cor 6:20). This transition, at least for me, was not a one-time experience, or a" Damascus Road" experience that happened in an instant, but a daily choice to decide if I am going to live for myself and my pleasures or for God and His purpose. A choice that too many times I've made incorrectly, but God hasn't wavered or given up on me.

As you choose Christ daily, things happen and things change. Your major worries lessen. Peace and joy consume you. Anxieties cease. You want to live to please God. You want to be intimate with your Father and Savior. You seek God to reveal your purpose in your life to influence and change the kingdom. Yes, as dads our biggest discipleship opportunity is to point our kids to Christ. That is the most important gift you can give your kids. But I don't think that is all God has planned for you. What is stopping you from seeking and asking God to show you your purpose for the short life He gave you on this Earth? Is it pride? Is it busyness? Are you concerned that He might challenge a lifestyle choice that has you not living your fullest? He will. Are you afraid that God is going to call you to Africa? He might. What if he needs you right where you are currently? In the marketplace as a Christian business leader. In your kid's schools as a volunteer or coaching your kid's flag football game. As an encourager to others on your morning walk in your neighborhood or during your kid's basketball games. No need to overthink this. Take where you are now in life and ask God what you can do to become a light for Him. He will show you.

Sitting here early on this Sunday morning, I just received a text from my buddy Mat Tilley saying, "This world is temporary, so how are we living for eternity with Him? I must come to the foot of the cross and surrender knowing I can never be good enough, but He is perfect." Yes!! Mat gets it. Quick backstory on Mat, he owns a business that picks up trash at apartments. Sounds pretty sexy, right? His mission for his business is to honor and portray Christ in the marketplace. This isn't always the most popular stance and exposes him to naysayers, but once you meet him, you see and know that this is the core of who he is. He has fully surrendered and is all in for his purpose!

It's time to surrender it all Dadvoted reader. Once you accept your spiritual "YOLO" as **"You Only Living for One,"** it shifts even further to a deeper "YOLO," as **"You Only Live in Obedience."** That's what God wants. After He grabs your attention and you make Him the "One" in your life, now "obedience" links you to the Father and His purpose for you. You are connected to the One who can move mountains, who can take your underdog story and make you an overcomer. He just wants obedience.

I hope you hear the excitement in my words for you and your future. I fully believe that your best days are before you.

1 Cor 2:9 says, "What no eye has seen, what no ear has heard, and what no human mind has conceived–the things God has prepared for those who love him." I also know that God has great plans for you and your kids when he says in Jeremiah 29:11: "For I know the plans I have for you," declares the Lord, "plans to prosper you and not to harm you, plans to give you hope and a future." If you fully understand your purpose and are living in it, then it will naturally radiate out of you and your kids will notice. From there, you will be able to tell them what your purpose on Earth is other than raising them to know, love and trust Jesus. You will also be able to tell them that you are daily praying that God will reveal His purposes to them at an early age and that they will accept it and live in obedience to their calling. Plant the seed now, not only in Heavenly places, but also in your kid's heart. Water it in scripture and ask God to make it grow through prayer. Of course, for His kingdom use. Pray bold prayers for your future and for your kids. Ask God to show up and show off in their lives. My friend, don't miss this. **YOLO! "You Only Live for One," "You Only Live in Obedience!"**

MINDSET

THE MIND IS a powerful thing. In fact, the mind may be the most powerful influencer in your whole body. The way you think about yourself can and will affect the outcome in any situation and will determine your reaction(s) to that outcome. If you have doubts and believe that failure is an option, chances are that you are going to pursue things that will lead to that outcome, or even worse cause you to do nothing and continue to stay in a rut. Rapper NF speaks to this in his song "The Search" when he says:

> "The point I'm making is the mind is a powerful place
> And what you feed it can affect you in a powerful way
> It's pretty cool, right? Yeah, but it's not always safe
> Just hang with me, this will only take a moment, OK?
>
> Just think about it for a second, if you look at your face
> Every day when you get up and think you'll never be great
> You'll never be great – not because you're not, but the hate
> Will always find a way to cut you up and murder your faith"

Likewise, if you have a mindset of victory and positivity, even when you fail, you will see it as a growth opportunity. Though I'm naturally an optimist, I am also a realist in tough situations. For example, I just had two people walk from my operations team in the busiest time of our year. The realist side of me knows that this sucks really bad, and we are in a bind. The optimist side of me says that they weren't right for the job, and now we have an opportunity to find better talent and move the meter in our favor. Unfortunately, not all my team thinks that way, but as the leader, it is up to me to portray that and dive in and help shift that mindset. The same goes for being the leader of my household. If I outwardly portray doom and gloom because of my thoughts or reactions during tough situations, what do you think my boys are going to absorb? But if I am real and tell my boys that this situation, whatever it may be, stinks, but that we are going to persevere, get through it, and be stronger, I am being truthful, but building up a mindset of overcoming.

In business we talk a lot about a growth mindset vs. that of a fixed mindset. Carol S. Dweck wrote a book titled *Mindset*, which discusses in length her research and theory of a growth vs. fixed mindset and how it relates to all areas of life including personal and professional. In this she says: "It's not just our abilities and talent that brings us success but whether we approach them with a fixed or growth mindset." She also says, "A fixed mindset makes you concerned with how you will be judged: the growth mindset makes you concerned with improving." (Dweck, 2006)[6] The main point is that the way you think determines your actions, which shapes the course of your life. This doesn't begin as an adult, but is formed and molded when you are young by those around you, i.e., parents, teachers, coaches, etc. Your mindset will help or hinder you in your pursuit of your dreams and goals.

Let's shift this towards the mind of the believer. For those that have trusted Jesus as their Savior and are living for Him daily. What does this mean? What does the Bible say about the mind? It says in 1 Cor 2:16; "Who has known the mind of the Lord so as to instruct him?" "But we have the mind of Christ." Well, that's a gamechanger.

Not only do we have the Spirit of God living in us, but we have the mind of Christ? Let me say that again for emphasis. Not only do we have the Spirit of God living in us, we also have the mind of Christ! So, if we have the mind of Christ, how should we react? We should think and react like Jesus. Having the spirit and the mind of Christ gives us power. Does that give us an unfair advantage? You are dang right it does and it's a gift! We have the Creator's power engrained in us. It's in our DNA as we become a new creation in Christ. I feel like I need to scream out the famous song by Snap, "I've got the Power!" Where we – emphasis on me – deviate, is that we still have moments of self-dependance. We are determined to muscle through with sheer grit and determination. Don't get me wrong, I believe that is needed, but if we pair that with God's power that lives in us, we are mentally unstoppable.

The world we live in today thrives on selling doom and gloom or unleashing unnecessary fear about "what may happen." This is why I try my best to stay away from TV, especially the local news and all the political outlets. What we put into our mind will translate into our thoughts, actions and reactions. I'm not immune to the problems of this world or keep my head in the clouds on purpose to "run away" or not notice all the issues in front of us as a society. But I do know this: I've read the end of the Bible and I know who wins in the end! I take this confidence (aka faith) and daily pursue the Lord in scripture so that He gives me more hope. The Bible says, "Do not conform to the pattern of this world but be transformed by the renewing of your **mind**. Then you will be able to test and approve what God's will is – His good pleasing and perfect will" (Rom 12:2). This is a daily renewing for me. Each day, I lay down my agenda, my thoughts, the world's view and seek the King asking him to renew my mind; to give me His thoughts, His agenda and His view. I recently heard my good friend and Pastor Bryan Shippey speak on the patterns in our life and he referenced the verse above. He gave a new perspective that I had never thought about. He said that when we become believers, God gives us a new heart, but we keep the same mind. Wow! Never thought about it this way. He continued to speak and urged us to renew our mind so that our patterns in life would be that of Jesus' patterns so that the people around us would see firsthand the goodness of God and that He would be glorified.

Dadvoted reader, our kids are looking to us for guidance not just on practical things but on the mental as well. Start speaking growth mindset specifics in their lives by both your words and actions. If your mind isn't in a good place or you tend to go negative, reset your patterns. Turn to the Father and ask him to renew your mind and give you His thoughts. Remember, you have the mind of Christ.

MESSY AND ORDINARY

THERE'S A MISNOMER that you are not usable by God until you have it all figured out; that He's looking for people who have it all together. People that both inwardly and outwardly must portray some sort of ultimate standard of Godliness and perfection before God can use you for His purposes. This is a lie from the enemy and is not the case. This is also a false and unattainable expectation that will paralyze you from moving in your identity – again, a weapon of the enemy. God uses all types of people in all phases of their spiritual walk. The timeline of transformation for each believer is different and some more radical than others. For example, Saul killed Christians and hated Jesus. He was met on the rode to Damascus by the Lord where his eyesight was taken away. Three days later Jesus sent Ananias to heal Saul when He said: "Go! This man is my chosen instrument to proclaim my name to the Gentiles and their kings and to the people of Israel" (Acts 9:15). God restored Saul's eyesight, changed his name to Paul, and led him to become one of the figureheads in starting the early Church and writing majority of the New Testament. This radical transformation took place immediately taking Saul from killer to Kingdom warrior. Some transformations are not fast and take years, which I can attest to.

Throughout the Bible there are numerous occurrences of "messy people" being used to move the Kingdom further. In *The Purpose Driven Life*, Rick Warren says:

"Abraham was old, Jacob was insecure, Leah was unattractive, Joseph was abused, Moses stuttered, Gideon was poor, Samson was codependent, Rehab was immoral, David had an affair and all kinds of family problems, Elijah was suicidal, Jeremiah was depressed, Jonah was reluctant, Naomi was a widow, John the Baptist was eccentric, Peter was impulsive and hot tempered, Martha worried, the Samaritan woman had several failed marriages, Zacchaeus was unpopular, Thomas had doubts, Paul had poor health and Timothy was timid. This is quite a variety of misfits, but God used each of them in his service. He will use you too if you stop making excuses." (Warren, 2002)[7]

So, why did Jesus use messy people during his time on Earth? He used some of the messiest people to prove His point that <u>ALL</u> can come to Him. This is still true today. Not only were messy people used, but common, regular, often lowly people were accepted and used in major ways. Jesus didn't walk with the famous or the "religious leaders" of his day. He walked, met, and dined with some of the worst people based on the standards of that time and even today. Tax collectors, prostitutes, and swindlers accompanied Jesus. His first followers were common people like fishermen and construction workers. Jesus's methods drove the religious leaders of His day mad. They didn't understand why He would associate with the unclean and common especially if He was the Messiah as He claimed. They didn't understand that He had love in His heart for everyone and especially loved when they humbled themselves and turned from their old ways to that of God's ways.

I'd like to tell you a story of God moving in messy people that is close to my heart. I know someone very well who knew the Lord at any early age and used to lay in bed with worship music in his ears. He yearned to know the Lord more and did so during his High School years.

He had a basis of a foundation in college, which kept him being "just good enough," to not get caught, but wasn't fully dependent on Jesus. Early in his career he fought hard to move up corporately and did so pretty quickly. With this success came more self-reliance. He worked hard and he played hard. That was engrained in him by bosses, coworkers, and mentors. God was there, but not at the forefront. He got married and he and his wife joined a small group. He made the comment early on "if they only knew how I talked and what I did outside of church." This couple was asked to then lead a small group. And he thought, if they still only knew how I was when I wasn't at church. But they saw leadership skills in him and genuine care for people. Transformation started. Then they found themselves called to do High School ministry. Transformation continued as he was called to speak into kids' lives. He was all in. Then he moved back home to where family was and new neighbors, friends, and coworkers came into the picture. He loved the Lord, but addictions began to creep in. Slowly and not noticeable to the average person, but the stresses of the world wore on him. He loved the Lord and had a great small group and church but was lacking in that zeal and fervor for the Lord to surrender it all. The Lord didn't leave him. His income went up, he got the big job, self-reliance took over, but he still longed for the Lord and went back to meeting with Him daily. Transformation happened again, but full surrender still wasn't there. The world had a say and people pleasing and fitting in took precedence over pleasing Jesus. He went down a further path of addiction. Often meeting with the Lord or going to Sunday service with a hangover. He hated it, but it happened week after week. He hit his knees often and asked that the desires would depart, but they still kept coming. The enemy had his claws in him, but he looked great to the outside world. He was the "fun guy" and the one who rallied the troops. He was loved by all. He would meet with his small group and other accountability buddies and tell them that he had to stop, but the world kept winning. He loved the Lord, just wasn't ready to give up control. Then he was called to become a writer for the Kingdom. It intrigued him, but he sat on it for a solid year before being obedient to it. The Lord remained in Him. There was some fruit, but not full surrender. The book started and the content was good. It was from the Lord, but there still wasn't full surrender. The ups and downs of the world continued to win and there was always a bad day, a hard day, or a victorious day to let the world win and pull him away. Finally, he was nudged enough from personal conviction and prayers from a hurt spouse that longed for him to surrender so he could do great things in the Kingdom. On day 40 of sobriety, the word "Dadvoted" was given to him; was given to me. The Lord told me to wait on Him in my surrender and then He revealed it to me.

The Lord never gave up on me and he won't give up on you. He wants to see His people healed, redeemed, and restored. He wants them to live in the purpose He has set before them and thrive. The Lord uses the number 40 significantly in the Bible. The Israelites wandered for 40 years before they found the promised land. Moses was on the mountain for 40 days before receiving the Ten Commandments and Jesus fasted for 40 days before his ministry started. I wandered for 40 years similarly to the Israelites in the desert. The promise land was before me I just didn't want to release everything to the Lord. The Lord revealing my book title and brand to me after 40 days of obedience is no coincidence. By no means am I comparing my writing journey to that of Moses or Jesus, but to solidify the point that God does not give up on his people and wants to pour out His favor on us, especially when it comes to us surrendering for the advancement of the Kingdom. God wants messy people, who know they are messy, but are willing to humble themselves before Him so He can purify our mess and turn it into a message. Dadvoted reader, if you want to fully make an impact for the Kingdom and for your kids, ***surrender it all***. You know that one thing that is keeping you from living your fullest, most fruitful life that God has planned for you. Surrender it today! It's so worth it!

QUIET TIME

MEETING WITH THE Lord daily is a game changer if you want to reach Dadvotedness at its peak. To be able to set the tone for your day by praying, reading the word, doing a devotional and worshipping God isn't just a spiritual discipline, but necessary to connecting with God to tackle each day. There isn't a magic formula, other than to do it! Even if you start small like with five minutes and build from there is still better than not doing anything at all. I understand that some of you aren't morning people, or your schedule doesn't allow much time to start in the morning, but my challenge for you is to really dig deep and evaluate all possible reasons why you can't give God the first portion of your day.

Meeting with God first sets the tone for your day – If you start with God's word and seeking His face, you are more likely to be calmer through the day. You are more likely to think before you speak or take a breath before you react to a situation. You are more likely to see the good in a person or be more understanding out the gate.

Meeting with God first puts you on the right track – If you meet with God first thing you are more than likely going to make better decisions throughout the day. Just like if I work out first thing in the morning (after my time with the Lord), I am more likely to make better food decisions throughout the day as I don't want to ruin the hard work I put I in earlier.

Meeting with God first allows you to give Him your best – We are usually whooped dogs at the end of the day. I try and pray at night right when I turn the lamp off but am usually conked out within a few minutes or I just pray a very simple prayer. I'm not on my knees intervening for God to move at 10 pm at night like I am first thing in the morning.

Meeting with God first satisfies your soul – I have a buddy, David, in a community group and he gave the following visual. Think if you start your day without any breakfast and right out the gate you are faced with a twinkie and then another twinkie and you pass up another twinkie. That twinkie is a temptation that your body may resist at first, but the more you see or think about that twinkie, the more likely you are going to succumb to that twinkie, which will make you feel bad or sick. Now if you start out by nourishing your body with a wholesome meal of eggs, oatmeal, and fruit, that twinkie isn't a temptation to you at all. That is like fueling your body with God first thing in the morning. The day's temptations are much easier to resist which keeps you aligned on God's path.

For us church goers, we've heard about the importance of reading the Bible and prayer for years. It's been engrained and driven into us time and time again. If that's the case, then why aren't we consistently doing it? I'm not trying to be legalistic here either or make you have a spiritual checklist where you check your daily quiet time box to feel like a super Christian. It's still a matter of the heart. My prayer is that you would have a desire to meet with God to grow closer to Him, and to hear from Him through His word or from Him speaking to you.

Most of us are getting between six and seven hours of sleep per night, meaning we have around 18 hours of the day spent awake. Can we not give at least $1/36^{th}$ of our day (2.78 percent if you do 30 minutes) to the creator of the universe?

I can speak from experience that it is the richest time of my day and that I feel different if I skip it. I must drink from His well daily for my soul to be satisfied, or I'm going to find something that will satisfy my soul that is usually temporary or harmful to me. Salt water doesn't satisfy and will never satisfy me on a hot day of doing yard work in August in Texas. But ice-cold water in a metal thermos quenches deep into my soul. That's the same as meeting with God daily. Now, I'd be lying if I didn't say there are some days that my mind is wandering; I rush it, or I flat out skip it. But I always come back to it. Make it a routine that you don't miss. In fact, right now I want to pray for you and your time meeting with the Lord.

> *Lord, I pray for my Dadvoted reader right now. I pray that You would give him the passion to meet consistently with You, to set up a daily routine, unhurried, so that he can seek You, understand You more, and feel Your love. I pray that You reveal immediately what this looks like and that You pour out Your spirit of discipline on him so that he stays with that routine. Remove the roadblocks the enemy has setup or is trying to setup to hinder this precious time with You. I pray that You will speak to the reader early and often through Your Word and Your Spirit so that his soul would yearn for more of You.*

I pray that through this time there would be transformation and not just information transfer. That this wouldn't be a spiritual exercise to check a box, but the richest time of the day that will set the tone and direction for his day and more importantly straighten his path. My biggest prayer would be that this time would change him to be a better man, husband, and father and that his kids will see this and model it all the days of their lives. Thank you, Lord, for the privilege of getting to meet with You. May it bless us so that we can be a blessing. In Jesus name, Amen!

TRUE MANHOOD

WHAT DEFINES A true man? For those with boys, how you portray this foundational truth to your son(s) will determine so much in his life. Ignoring this is an option, but your inaction will reflect in your son, and most likely allow someone or something else to align their views onto him. Likewise, if you provide or confirm the worldly view of manhood, you son's view will be skewed and bathed in lies. The worldview has it backwards yet again on what manhood really is and what it looks like when embodied correctly. At the core, true manhood is far from what is spoken to your son, but what is lived out in your life as a Dadvoted father. How you act, respond and live will stick with them forever and serve as their model. Lot of pressure? Somewhat. Does that perk you up or make you nervous? I hope so!

Let's break it down on what True Manhood is and conversely what it isn't:

True Manhood has a firm foundation of faith built upon the redeeming love of Jesus. You know that you are made by God, in His image. You know that you were bought with a price and that Jesus redeemed you on the cross. Nothing can shake you. When the waves of life hit you, you stand firm.

Strong and courageous – This isn't just physical strength, but mental and spiritual as well. You know the Lord is with you wherever you go. You walk in faith, knowing that the Lord has cleared a path for you, and that He is also beside you.

Knows purpose and identity in Christ – You know what God has called you here on Earth to do (purpose) and you know how He views you (identity). Not many know this, or they generically have created something in their mind which may or may not be positive. This is the ultimate gamechanger and God wants to reveal this to His people. If you don't know, start seeking the Lord now to reveal both to you.

Loves the Bible – Knows that this is the authoritative word of God. Obeys it. Even the hard verses.

Meets with Jesus – Everyday, unhurried, passionately pursues God.

Prays like crazy – Believes prayer is the real work, that God hears and answers pray, and is moving today.

Dies to self daily – Isn't self-seeking, but seeks to help others and add value to others each day.

Humble in spirit – Stays calm, isn't flashy, doesn't name drop to get recognition, status doesn't matter, doesn't have to have the last word, doesn't try to one up or outdo other stories.

Spirit Led – Leans on Jesus to guide path and footsteps. Doesn't make a big decision without bathing it in prayer.

Builds spiritual foundation for family – His family knows Jesus because he talks about Him. Prays over, with and for family. Initiates prayer time with spouse and family. Doesn't miss church unless he is out of town. Doesn't let kid's activities take away from church. Uses the Bible to talk about life, issues, problems and to show how this book is the source of all answers.

Big Worshiper – Sings and praises for an audience of One, the true King

No Idols – Only Worships Jesus. Doesn't have anything that takes him away from Jesus. When gets off track, recognizes it and gets back quickly

Respects women – Sees women as precious daughters of Christ and not objects. Doesn't sleep around or believe that the more woman he has been with makes him more of a man. Protects them. His eyes don't wander.

Doesn't shy away from tough conversations – Talks to his kids about tough topics. Isn't embarrassed to talk about sex or the body with his kids. Is real with them. Tells them the truth. Is prepared.

Servant Heart – Seeks to serve others versus self. Strives to out serve wife. Serves kids and community.

Slow to become angry – Doesn't raise voice to draw attention or be heard. Gives the benefit of the doubt. Knows when to walk away before something regretful is spoken.

Encourages others– Big encourager. Sees the best in people and tells them this to instill it.

Corrects in love – Doesn't embarrass or call people out. Gently guides people when they have gone astray.

Controls Tongue – Speaks sincerely, speaks truth, speaks in love. Knows that words can cut deep and wound. Keeps mouth clean and doesn't use foul language. Doesn't slander, gossip, or tell off color jokes.

Integrity follows – Period, never a doubt. Especially when no one is around.

Self-aware – Knows that little eyes are watching and look up to him. Acknowledges mistakes and asks for forgiveness when he messes up. Works to use things as teaching moments.

Great Listener – Engages in active listening. Remembers people's names. Remembers what your wife tells you (this was added by Keeli).

Keeps up with people – Intentional. When he tells someone that they should go to lunch or coffee soon, he follows-up and does it.

Accountable and seeks accountability – Meets with guys to strengthen each other. Calls out a brother when he is blatantly sinning. Holds self extremely accountable.

Seeks to win, but not at all costs – Plays by the rules. Doesn't lie or cheat to advance. Holds head high in defeat. Doesn't gloat in victory. Praises God either way. Learns from losses, grateful in victory.

Is bold in faith– Not wishy washy – Walks the walk and talks the talk, isn't a chameleon trying to fit in with everyone.

Stands firm even when it's not popular – Not concerned about what people think or if they will ridicule him for being against the grain or against popular belief.

Disciplined – Works hard in all parts of life and not just at work.

Doesn't overindulge – Nothing has a stronghold on him, like food, porn, booze or gambling

Watches and listens to clean things – Knows that what he watches or listens to will influence his thoughts which will affect actions

Keeps track of spending – Doesn't let money consume him. Stays on budget. Disciplined in spending. Doesn't hide spending from spouse.

Always learning – Reads books, challenges self to learn something new

Spends time wisely – Doesn't take for granted this precious and depleting resource

Trustworthy–Can be trusted with both the little and big things

Is a steward and not an owner – Understands that nothing is his, but all is given from God and manages it well.

Treats his bride like the angel that she is – Still has the same passion and fervor for wife as when they were young. Take her on dates frequently. Surprises her with small gifts. Helps around the house. Dotes on her.

Accepts all People – Doesn't mean he agrees with them and all their choices, but accepts them nonetheless. Doesn't shy away from difficult people

Talks to people on their level – Doesn't try and sound smarter than everyone. Doesn't stand over or domineer people. Kneels down to talk to kids face to face, especially when disciplining them or teaching them something.

Doesn't see color – God created everyone in His image, and you believe that regardless of color or nation of origin.

Protects the weak – He knows there is no room for bullies.

Doesn't take freedom for granted – Respects country and those who fought for what we have.

Works to live, doesn't live to work – Work life balance is key. Is passionate about job, but doesn't allow work to be his identity.

Self-respect – Takes care of self. Fuels body correctly, exercises regularly, gets good rest.

Love for Nature – Respects God's creation. Shares adventures with kids and family in nature.

Generous – Big Giver. Not just money, but time, energy, and effort. Has joy when giving.

Shows emotion – Doesn't hide emotions. Hurts when others hurt.

Vulnerable – Doesn't wear a façade, is real. Knows weaknesses or blind spots.

Owns Mistakes – Doesn't point the finger at others. Learns from mistakes. Doesn't stew or condemn self.

Gives kids his best not his leftovers – Self explanatory

Is Fun – Is rambunctious with kids, creates fun games and inside family jokes. Is silly

Has Hope – Has hope in all things and situations. Knows the world is broken, but also knows the end of the Bible and that Jesus is coming back for His people. Doesn't let political nonsense or who the President is determine joy or peace. The stock market has no effect on his happiness. Sees the good in people and all situations, knowing that God works all things for good, even when hope looks bleak.

Dadvoted reader. Strive for these, live for these, pass these along to your sons, nephews, their friends and every young man that you encounter.

Challenge other dads by your actions as they see an upright man that embodies what True Manhood really is about.

COMPLAIN AMONGST YOURSELF

"**I LOVE WHEN** people complain," said no one ever! What type of people do you like to be around? Positive, glass half-full, optimistic, encouraging people? Or, do you prefer negative, glass half-empty, pessimistic, Eeyore's? We live in a negative world. A world where negative reviews, thoughts, and opinions flood the internet from everything to politics, school policies, religious views, and everything in between. Heck I even heard on the local news a lady called 911 because the restaurant messed up her order. Unreal!

Here are a few more ridiculous complaints provided by Buzzfeed.com:[8]

- "While working in retail many years ago, I had a customer complain to my manager that I was too happy while helping her, that she believed that I was actually being rude and insincere on purpose. I got a verbal warning and a write-up."

- "A coworker hugged me when I gave her a birthday present. Later, I was pulled into my supervisor's office because someone reported us for "inappropriate PDA."

- "I'm a firefighter and had a citizen complaint. I wouldn't take my boots off while entering a lady's house. It is against our protocol to take off any of our safety gear. Her house was actively on fire when she made the request."

These are blatantly absurd and yes pulled off the internet, but I have a personal one that I experienced firsthand. I received a voicemail years ago from a lady requesting me to call her back immediately and that it was an emergency. I called her back and she told me that my installer had damaged her car. Of course, this was a big deal and I asked her to explain what happened. She then told me that my installer was blocking the road with a roll of carpet. She couldn't wait for him to get back down and move it, so she decided to "gun it" and try to jump the roll of carpet (I'm picturing *The Dukes of Hazzard*). When she did this, she got high centered and stuck on the roll of carpet. After they got her off the carpet her car was making a weird noise and she demanded that I pay her for the damage. Needless to say, I took down her information, kindly asked her to report that to her complex, hung up the phone and threw away her info.

I tell these stories because people are so quick to complain. Everyone feels wronged, or that people are out to get them, and it doesn't have to be this way. This "victim" mentality holds people back in life, in work and in relationships. No one likes a complainer. The Bible speaks to this as well saying, "Do everything without complaining and arguing, so that no one can criticize you. Live clean, innocent lives as children of God, shining like bright lights in a world full of crooked and perverse people" (Phil 2: 14-15 NLT).

A little self-check and self-reflection time. Are you quick to complain? Do you feel that you are being victimized? That's hard to self-diagnose, as I haven't met too many with the victim mentality who actually own up to it, as they don't see it. I challenge you to reflect on that, phone a friend, or ask your spouse. Hopefully they will alert you in truth and grace. And that your reaction wouldn't solidify your state of being a victim but the beginning of a new self-awareness. Do you let little things annoy you? I get it, service is at an all-time low, and our expectations are at an all-time high. Post pandemic, we have been pushed into a new norm of acceptance. Some of it forced and a lot of it created by people. And less is not more when it comes to customer service. But we are also part of the problem as we live in the "get it now, instant gratification era," and create a lot of our own internal drama when we don't get our way. What about when someone does something nice for you, do you shoot it down? Do you think how it could have been done better, or do you accept the kind act? The litmus test for me today and always will be Jesus. How did He respond? How did He react? Did He complain? What was His reaction when people actually were out to get Him? What led Him and can that lead me as well? Jesus had the Spirit of God upon Him and He was here with purpose to do the Lord's work. That same spirit He possessed from God has also been passed to us as a gift to all who believe. He speaks further to this in John 14:25-26 saying, "All this I have spoken while still with you. But the Advocate, the Holy Spirit, whom the Father will send in my name, will teach you all things and will remind you of everything I have said to you."

As believers, we have the Holy Spirit living in us. We can accept to live in the Spirit or not. The choice is ours. Because we have this freedom to choose is also why I see so many believers on Sunday worshiping, but on Monday living in fear, doubt, debauchery and in a constant state of unhappiness with a complaining heart. When we don't live by the Spirit as a believer, the Bible says that we have a form of godliness, but no power. 2 Timothy 3:2-5 says, "People will be lovers of themselves, lovers of money, boastful, proud, abusive, disobedient to their parents, ungrateful, unholy, without love, unforgiving, slanderous, without self-control, brutal, not lovers of God, treacherous, rash, conceited, lovers of pleasure rather than lovers of God – having a form of godliness but denying its power. Have nothing to do with such people." Ouch on a lot of levels. I don't think any of us want these traits spoken when someone asks to describe us.

So how do we rid ourselves of all this and live for God? And how do we know when we are living in the Spirit? First, we must completely surrender to God. We must daily meet with Jesus and ask Him to soften our hearts, to forgive us of our sinful patterns and shortcomings and confess these things to Him. Ask Him to renew our minds and transform our hearts. For Him to give us His eyes to see the world and how He views people, and for Him to break our hearts for what breaks His. Open the Bible daily and ask God to speak to you through His word. Get consistent in going to church and get involved in a community group or small group or men's group. You can't do this alone. This is a process. It takes time, energy, and effort, but is so worth it. So how do you know when you are living in the Spirit? There is fruit. Yes, fruit. Gal 5:22-23 (ESV) says, "But the fruit of the Spirit is love, joy, peace, patience, kindness, goodness, faithfulness, gentleness, and self-control." This fruit is most seen and put on center stage when you react differently than the world would to a problem. You are calm and you stay calm, you have joy deep within and don't waiver based on if you are getting your way. Your words build up and aren't harsh, even when people are being ridiculous. You are kind to the unkind. You love the hard to love, not just the ones that love you.

Dadvoted reader, I say this a lot, but your kids are watching you. Do you complain when your server is slow or messes up your order? It's ok to be disappointed, but do you have to win and prove yourself? How do you react when people are idiots on the road in front of your kids? Confession here, I'm not the most fruitful on the kill or be killed roads in Houston Texas. Do you bring your work home and complain about the people at work or do you leave it in your car? Are you vocal about politics, the stock market, the price of gas and food, complaining and stripping peace out of your heart and your household? We (myself included) have to do a better job. I fully believe that negativity breeds negativity. Let's show our kids that we can stay calm, that we don't complain and worry because we are so connected to the Spirit that our fruit is apparent for all to see. This will shift a generation of complainers to conquerors!

"YOU GOT TO PRAY JUST TO MAKE IT TODAY"

MC HAMMER NAILED it back in 1990 with this jam. Most wouldn't know, but this song was his most successful and reached #2 on the Billboard 100 where "You Can't Touch This" only made it to #8. Thirty-two years later this song title is a mantra for me, and I hope that it is or will become for you. As we say and believe at my local church, prayer is the real work. Programs are great and needed, ministry is vital, outreach shows God's people being the hands and feet of Christ, small groups build community and accountability, but without prayer these amount to nothing but spiritual activities and often become stale.

Prayer shows our obedience to call upon the creator of the heavens and the earth to access His power and to bring Heaven to Earth. This isn't calling upon the Lord for just your needs, but to unlock His will for your life while softening your heart to everything around you. It shows dependance and is necessary not only for growth but to sustain confidence in Christ while we are placed in a failing society and world. So, what keeps us from fully utilizing this free resource? Unfortunately, our independence, self-reliance, affluent status, natural freedom, and safety that most of us have being an American has us in a comfortable state, which is where the enemy wants to keep us. We aren't facing extreme persecution; we aren't worried about our next meal and often are concerned about what others think than what the Lord wants for us. The Lord is yearning for His people to not just become followers, but to become intimates. Intimates then become ambassadors. But to become an intimate of anyone, you must have a deep relationship built on love and trust, and to get there you must meet with that person a lot. Spending precious time with that person; at the core, that is what prayer is. It's a continued conversation with God. It's not a ritual, but I do recommend that you have a quiet place that you meet daily with the Lord in prayer and meditation. Apart from that, prayer is a conversation throughout the day with your friend, who also happens to be the Savior of the world. I hope this type of intimacy would be a goal and honor to obtain, and that prayer wouldn't be another spiritual item on your checklist or something when you are in need.

When you pray, how are you praying? Is it a repetitive prayer that you pray every day? A rushed prayer before dinner to bless the food because you are starving, or at night real quick to get your kids to bed? I'm not immune myself to these types of prayers and have to consciously be very intentional when it comes to praying. Is prayer boring to you? Or do you not have a prayer life at all? Some tough questions indeed, but let me challenge and encourage you to pursue prayer at all costs. Prayer is a privilege. To be able to approach Jesus and pour your heart out to Him is something that we shouldn't take lightly or for granted. Humbly calling upon the name of Jesus to hear your cry for help, change, healing, redemption or to show up in a situation that is dire is what God wants. He wants to hear from His people and know that they need Him. It's also a matter of the heart and not the head. I think of the parable of the Pharisee and tax collector in Luke 18 when Jesus says:

"Two men went to the Temple to pray. One was a Pharisee, and the other was a despised tax collector. The Pharisee stood by himself and prayed this prayer: 'I thank you, God, that I am not like other people – cheaters, sinners, adulterers. I'm certainly not like that tax collector! I fast twice a week, and I give you a tenth of my income.'

But the tax collector stood at a distance and dared not even lift his eyes to heaven as he prayed. Instead, he beat his chest in sorrow, saying, 'O God, be merciful to me, for I am a sinner.' I tell you, this sinner, not the Pharisee, returned home justified before God. For those who exalt themselves will be humbled, and those who humble themselves will be exalted."

Those whose heart is desperate for God and who fervently pray will see miracles, will hear from God and will unleash peace throughout any circumstance or situation. I urge you Dadvoted reader to pray. How do you start or what is the formula? Not sure if there is such a formula, but mirroring the Lord's prayer is a good place to start. I'm not going back against my repetitive comment stated above, as I do believe in saying the Lord's prayer, but let's follow the pattern to give us direction in our prayer life.

"Our Father in heaven hallowed be your name"

Open by praising the name of Jesus. Tell him how good He is and what He means to you. Thank Him for saving you, giving freedom, and eternal life. Stand in awe of Him. Use scripture back at Him like "Who am I that you are mindful of me" (Psalms 8:4) and thank him that he knows you personally – "you know the number of hairs on my head" (Matt 10:30). Soak in His love for you.

"Your Kingdom come, Your will be done, on earth as it is in Heaven."

Pray that God would show up and show off in your life and those around you. That the Kingdom of Heaven would invade Earth. That you would see your friends, neighbors, kids and their friends come to know Christ and live for Him. That communities would be changed, lives redeemed, all the hurt in the world abolished and that it would all point back to Jesus.

"Give us today our daily bread"

Provide for us today, Father. Not just with food, but with your Spirit. May we not worry about anything as your word proclaims that you feed the birds and cloth the fields with flowers, and that we are so much more important to you than those things. May we be a light to everyone around us, full of gratitude for what we have, knowing that "every good and perfect gift is from above" (James 1:17). May people see our joy and ask where it comes from, and we proclaim from You.

"And forgive us our debts as we also have forgiven our debtors"

God, thank You that you are a big forgiver! Thank You that You paid the ultimate price and died for me long before I knew You and that You died for ALL my sins, past, present, and future. That my sins have been removed and I have been made white as snow (Isaiah 1:18). And that You have forgotten my sins as far as the east is from the west (Psalm 103:12). Open my eyes and heart to anything I am doing that isn't from You and needs to be removed. Thank You that You've taught me to forgive and may I always be a big forgiver like You.

"And lead us not into temptation, but deliver us from the evil one."

Lord, protect us. We know the enemy wants us to stray from you, wants us to mess up or just wants us to be too busy to call upon you." Remove him! There is no place for him in my life or in my home. Thank you that we know the end of the story and that you will overthrow him, but for now, I will continue to trust you. If I am tempted, I will remember that you used scripture to fight off the attacks and so will I. I know that if I am tempted beyond what I can bear that You will provide a way out (1 Corinthians 10:13).

"For Yours is the kingdom, the power and glory."

Everything is Yours Jesus. May I live today and each day for You, Your will, and Your purpose. May I point people to You in every facet of my life and may I never compartmentalize and separate You from anything I am involved in. May Your love radiate through me to reach everyone I am in contact with. Use me how You wish today. May I be extremely aware of Your presence and Your promptings. Draw people closer to You, so they will be forever changed!

From here you can pray for your family, your needs and for others in your life. Pray with expectancy, knowing that God will show up, somehow or some way. Continue to pray these types of prayers throughout the day, more or less conversationally with Jesus. Pray for victories, thank him for struggles, knowing that He is going to redeem them for good and for your growth. Thank Him throughout the day for all the good in your life, both big and small.

Dadvoted reader, are you in for upping your game in prayer? Let's shift a bit to our kids. There are three specific prayer activities to engage in for the betterment of them.

Praying for your Kids

Here, we get to approach the throne of God to pray specifically over our kids. Prayer topics include praying for their salvation, their future, their purpose in life, their friends, and even their future spouse. Don't hold back! Ask the King to pour out blessings and favor over them. Pray for their protection and purity. Pray that God will use them for great things to further the Kingdom and point people to Jesus. To give them a massive platform to proclaim Christ! Be bold here! The stakes are too high!

Praying with your Kids

How else are your kids going to learn to pray and become comfortable praying if you don't pray with them? We like to get together on Sunday nights and "regroup" as a family. We discuss the week ahead and then ask for prayer requests. From there we all go around and pray for the specific needs that were just discussed and ask God to bless our week ahead.

Praying over your Kids

There is not a stronger way to proclaim and embed the things of God into your kids than to powerfully pray over them. To call upon Jesus with them and pray greatness over their lives. This is very similar to the topic above on praying for your kids, but here you make those requests not only known to God, but also known to your child. They will feel your love fully. Also, the Bible says, "where two or three gather in my name, there am I with them" (Matt 18:20). This will activate God's power over their life. Pray that God will fill them with His spirit and use them. That the enemy has no place or strength over you kids and that the gifts God has given them will be used to glorify the King.

Dadvoted reader, let's pray, not only to make it today, but to thrive today!

WHY DO I DO WHAT I DON'T WANT?

THIS IS A tough one. Why do I continue to do what I don't want to do? I have a couple of thoughts, but my main hope is to ease your angst and guide you. The apostle Paul, who, next to Jesus, is the key guy in the New Testament, not only starting the early church, but who also wrote majority of the New Testament. He experienced the most radical transformation in the Bible and suffered so much for the advancement of the Kingdom. When you read his writings, you are in awe of his perseverance, grit, passion and love for Jesus and the Gospel. You assume that after his conversion and meeting Jesus face to face, that he angelically floated through life and didn't struggle with the things that we struggle with on the daily. That's actually the complete opposite of the truth. In Romans 7 verse 15 he said, "I do not understand what I do. For what I want to do I do not do, but what I hate I do." Also, in 1 Cor 10:13 continues by saying, "No temptation has overtaken you except what is common to mankind." Hopefully that lightens your burden. One of the strongest figures of the New Testament who devoted the second half of his life to the Kingdom had struggles. Common struggles. Did things that he was ashamed of and had some tendencies to repeat them. This by no means gives you a hall pass to keep on making mistakes but should bring peace knowing that we all have issues and have to uncover them and work to understand why they continue to come again and again.

My first explanation of this simply is sin. I know you may be thinking that this is the cop out, easy answer or churchy response, but at the core of every one of us is a sin problem. Sin is the root of every misstep we make. If churches ever stop preaching on sin, then they will be missing the mark and doing a disservice to the people. Our sin problem must be addressed often as it is part of our DNA. Paul goes on saying in Romans 7:17, "As it is, it is no longer I myself who do it, but it is sin living in me. For I know that good itself does not dwell in me, that is, in my sinful nature." In verse 20 he continues with, "Now if I do what I do not want to do, it is no longer I who do it, but it is sin living in me that does it." As I continue to drive this in further, I am not trying to make you lose hope, but I will bring it full circle, I promise. We all have a sin problem and need to face that reality. Think of a small child snatching a toy away from another child. We parents didn't have to teach them that action, rather it was already engrained in them from birth.

So how do we get this sin problem in check? Maybe getting it in check is not a long-term solution, rather striving to be fully aware and deciding what are you going to feed and nurture. As a believer, you have the Spirit of God living inside you. You must decide what you will be a slave to, either the Spirit inside, or your flesh. Rom 8: 5-6 says, "Those who live according to the flesh have their minds set on what the flesh desires; but those who live in accordance with the Spirit have their minds set on what the Spirit desires. The mind governed by the flesh is death, but the mind governed by the Spirit is life and peace." The spirit and the flesh will always be in constant battle against each other. If you choose to live by the flesh, you will be an enemy of God and in a state of radical selfishness. But if you live by the Spirit and set your mind on the things of the Spirit, the desires of the flesh will subside as you continue to choose life in the Spirit. So, to answer the sin problem in a churchy way, yes, Jesus is the answer. He died for your sins, and my sins so that we could live in peace and freedom. But what we often miss from a deeper standpoint is that the same Spirit that raised Christ from the dead lives in us as believers. We can confidently walk in the Spirit and the flesh will become less fleshy. *Thank you, Jesus, for this hope and confidence in Your promise and for the gift of Your Spirit!*

My second explanation for why we do what we don't want has nothing to do with us individually. It stems around the concept of generational sin. These are sin patterns inherited from generations past that continue to linger in your family from generation to generation, decade to decade. Maybe you've never thought about this, or maybe your thought is, "well that's not fair." I want you to really consider this and if you have something that you are struggling with that you can't control, look back to your parents and your grandparents and see if those patterns were present in your childhood or before that you may have heard about. Anger, alcoholism, divorce, abuse, imprisonment are a few major ones that come to mind. What about other unseen or lessor diagnosed issues like, overspending, compulsive lying, negativity, slander or gossip. Did this run in your family? Do you struggle today with some of these same issues that are becoming or have become a stronghold in your life. There's a high likelihood that you have inherited this as a generational sin and chances are the enemy has had this stronghold in place for many years.

The good news is that these can be broken once you have full awareness and want to end the generational curse. How does this take place? It comes from a heart of repentance. Repentance is defined as changing the way you think. It's also a 180-degree turn from where you have been. Breaking this cycle through prayer and repentance personally is just a start though. You must also press into God and ask Him to forgive all the generations before you that suffered with and created this generational sin in you. Then, plead with God to release you from this generational curse and remove the stronghold that has overtaken you so that it will no longer live in you or be transferred to your kids. I can speak from experience that this is life changing and the start to reshaping your path and the path of your kids. It is refreshing and empowering and resets the bar for you and your kids, knowing that they won't suffer with the same things that have held you back for years. Deep inside, you already know what sin or sins are generational in nature and if you are feeling a nudge, that is most likely the Spirit convicting you to pray now and ask for the release of this generational curse. If so, let me lead you in this prayer:

> *God, we come to You today, knowing that You are good and You are the ultimate healer. We know that You want the best for Your people and want strongholds to be broken so that full transformation can happen, and You can work in us and through us to bring Heaven to Earth and advance Your Kingdom. The enemy is crafty, and he sometimes gets his claws into our family long before we are even born and digs in causing repeated sin and shame from generation to generation. But we also know that You redeem and renew, and that no stronghold is ever beyond Your reach, and no one is ever too far gone for You. Today we approach the throne of grace and ask You to move like never before in our lives. I pray for this reader and the generational sin of (Name the sin(s)) that has been in his family for years and kept many in bondage.*

*We ask for forgiveness of that sin dating back gen-
eration after generation before the reader may have
even been born. We pray that You would forgive the
parents, grandparents, great grandparents and this
reader and fully remove this generational curse from
them. We ask this in Your mighty name, not just to
heal this reader, but so that this curse would stop and
not be transferred through his kids. Lord, we believe
that You hear our prayers and You are moving these
mountains right now in heavenly places so that this
reader and his kids are free from this generational
sin. May this prayer give this reader new confidence
in You, and may You release all guilt and shame that
has accompanied him for years. Thank You that You
hear our cries for help and that You move!*

I am excited to hear the stories of generational strongholds that
will be broken. Please email me at dadvoted@gmail.com so I can
hear testimonies of God moving. I also encourage you to share your
struggles with you kids if they are of the appropriate age. I have
done this with my boys, and I have such peace knowing that these
strongholds have been removed from my family lineage. We won't
forget where we've been, but more importantly we won't forget God
showing up in our darkness and bringing forth light. Dadvoted
reader, we've got to stop the pattern of sinful living and selfish ways
in our own lives if we want to see our kids grow up to live a life of
substance and truth. Jesus will break chains and release the bondage
of guilt and shame if you are willing to surrender.

PATH TO SUCCESS

Success is something that most all men strive for. We want to win, we want to be recognized as successful, and we want success to follow us in every aspect of our life. How is that obtainable? Sheer grit? Working harder than everyone else? A little luck along the way? Those are key determinants towards achieving success, but scripture does what it normally does and gives us a very easy, but difficult response. I find it in Joshua 1:8 where it says, "Keep this Book of the Law always on your lips; meditate on it day and night, so that you may be careful to do everything written in it. Then you will be prosperous and successful."

I say easy but difficult because it seems like a straightforward approach. Read the Bible and you will be prosperous and successful. You may be thinking, "I can do that. In fact, I already do that a little bit, so I'm on the right path." But the difficulty comes when you actually go back, read, and absorb every word.

"Keep the Book of the Law always on your lips"–If it's on your lips, that means that you know it and speak it. It's not just hidden in your heart or in your head. You know the word. This doesn't mean that you exactly quote every word and throw in the book, chapter, verse, translation and then mic drop everyone. I would actually frown against that. But your words are rooted and bathed in scripture. How you view and respond to the world and to people is different than the average bear. When you respond, it has depth and reason and is not just emotional in context. Also, the verse said to <u>always</u> have it on your lips. Not just here and there, but always. You see the difficulty here? How often do our own words, ideas and agendas stay on our lips? Hard to keep the Word on your lips when we got so much other stuff vying for that space.

"Meditate on it day and night" – Think deeply about scripture day and night? Is that possible? I think this piggybacks on praying without ceasing. This is hard to physically do but can become more natural over time. With Jesus at the center of your life, you begin to talk to Him a lot and His word begins to flow through your thoughts. This takes time and intentionality without a doubt, and I'll be the first to admit, that I need improvement here. Very difficult indeed.

"So that you may be careful to do everything written in it." – Well now you're smoking something! I have to do <u>everything</u> written in it? There are some tough verses. I have to "consider it pure joy when I face a trial?" I have to "love my enemy?" This was written thousands of years ago. Does it still apply today? Then I remember 2 Timothy 3:16: "All Scripture is God-breathed and is useful for teaching, rebuking, correcting, and training in righteousness." The difficulty meter is increasing rapidly.

"Then you will be prosperous and successful" – So if I do this, I'm going to be rich and achieve success? Well depends on how you define prosperous and successful versus how God does. Yes, God may bless you with a lot of money. But I think this also speaks to your soul being prosperous. You won't worry so much, and you will be filled with peace and joy. Successful could also mean that you will see a lot of fruit around you. That you will see your kids grow to be spiritually mature, that your marriage will be successful and thriving and your career will flourish. This opens you up to so much flow and freedom in life, at home, and at your work and will guide you to make better decisions, which will lead to more success. I also believe that God will open unopenable doors for His believers that are following His will, way, and words. This leads to Godly success which may or may not lead to tangible success that the world is used to acknowledging. If God does bless you financially, you have a different mindset around the blessing as you know that it is a gift and is to be used wisely.

I hope you don't find this ask in Joshua too difficult or overwhelming causing you to shut down. God wants our best but isn't expecting our perfection or us to follow rigid rules. God is not a taskmaster. He wants open hearts that yearn to absorb His word so that He can reveal things to his believers, like dreams, passions, and opportunities. Don't close up here, because this seems unobtainable. All things are possible with God (Matt 19:26).

Is your life today following the path above for success? I'm not here to call you out but to challenge you. I've loved Jesus for over 25 years, but just recently discovered this true path to success. I lived for myself, my visions, my achievements with a little Jesus sprinkled alongside. I had some wins along the way, but they were shallow in nature and never truly fulfilling. That bonus check was allocated and spent before it even hit the account. The record year celebration lasted a brief moment just to be presented an even bigger more overwhelming goal for the next year. Building it bigger, better and faster in the name of profits led to more anxiety and stress. Turning to God's path of success changed everything and it followed me. The calmer and less stressed I became, the more it flowed to my team and my family. The more I leaned on God, the more the anxiety ceased. My business became a ministry and not grudging act. My celebrations of victory were sweeter, and my defeats were learning opportunities that I didn't stew in but dusted myself off quicker and moved on.

Dadvoted reader, we need to shift what the path of success looks like. Your success at your job shouldn't determine everything else in your life. Your work should be your ministry. Your home life shouldn't suffer because of your work. And neither should your spiritual life. All three should be lined up with God and His word and you will thrive. Yes, work hard at your job and strive to do well. You are wired for that. But you are also wired to work hard at home and for God. Let's include God in all areas of your life so that you will have Godly success and prosperity in God's eyes.

THE PRESENT OF THE PRESENT

*"Yesterday is history, tomorrow is a mystery, but today
is a gift of God, which is why it is called the present."*
Bill Keane

SO MANY OF us men are stuck. We are stuck because of our past:
our past decisions, past mistakes, past hurts. We constantly replay
our lives in our mind knowing what we should have done better, or
not done at all. Bitterness is harbored, anger burns within, or regret
sits at our doorstep. Or maybe it's the opposite. You reminisce about
the good ole days. Before there were so many responsibilities, bills
and adulting. Before kids and works deadlines sucked the life out
of you. Back when you were a little bit leaner and a lot meaner. A 9
pm bedtime didn't even cross your mind. You had very little worries.
Life was easy. There was no such thing as a "Dad Bod"!

Now some of us are stuck in the future. We worry about what is
going to happen. Who is going to be elected, what the stock market
is going to do, what inflation is going to look like, what college your
kids are going to get into, if you are going to lose your hair, and on
and on. You drain so much emotional energy on the "what if's" in
life. If you had a nickel for every time you had a "what if" scenario,
you'd be filthy rich. But then you'd worry about how to invest that
money and what if you made a bad decision and ended up like one
of those people who won the lottery and lost it all.

What does the bible say about the past? Isaiah 43:18 says, "forget about the former things; do not dwell on the past." What does the bible say about the future? Mathew 6:34 says, "Therefore do not worry about tomorrow, for tomorrow will worry about itself. Each day has enough trouble of its own." Why do we do this to ourselves? We are only promised today. Today is a gift. If we dwell in the past or worry about the future, we are wasting today. How do we address this? I tend to lean on the only one who transcends time. Hebrews 13:8 says, "Jesus Christ is the same yesterday and today and forever." So even though we are changing, Jesus never does. He renews us, regenerates us, refreshes us as we seek Him and keep our eyes on Him. If we are connected to Him, we don't have regrets of our past, because we know that we have been cleansed. We don't miss the good old days, because we know that our best days are before us. We are aware of the future but know that it's a mystery and that God has our path established. We confidently rest in 1 Corinthians 2:9, "What no eye has seen, what no ear has heard, and what no human mind has conceived the things that God has prepared for those who love him."

Dadvoted reader, let's face each day as a new adventure. Our past is just that, our past. We have lived in it and through it and hopefully have learned from it. God has redeemed us from our past. The future is in God's hands. Regardless of who is in office, how the market performs or what laws are passed. I don't say this to mean that you should have a laissez faire attitude and not care about what's going on in society. But you shouldn't be shocked and surprised. You shouldn't get all worked up over everything coming across the news or heaven forbid social media. Live for today! Your kids want your intentionality today. They don't care about the past or the future. They just want a present dad in this present moment in time. Those moments one day won't exist. So maybe miss that

5:15 pm call when you are playing catch with your son. Reschedule that meeting so that you can do doughnuts and dads at the elementary school. Stop at your kids' school and surprise them for lunch. Your kids want you right now. Trust that Jesus will work out the future. Today is the one and only present you should open and be consumed with!

SECTION 2:
LIFE LESSONS

TEXAS FOOTBALL

IN TEXAS, HIGH school football is king. My hometown was the one you heard about that had 45,000 people in the town and the stadium held 40,000 (at least that's what it felt like). Friday nights, the town shut down and it was all about football. Our town needed two high schools, but that would split up the athletes and affect our team's success. Why would we do that? Our football coach was a legend and rumor had it, he made $1 less than the superintendent. That's Texas High School football for you. My goal though in writing about football is really related to the life lessons I learned growing up to that of which I must teach my boys regardless of if they ever step on the field and I challenge you to do the same for your kids.

What I didn't know 25 years ago were the valuable life lessons I was learning along the way and the leadership skills that were being engrained in me by some very caring and loving coaches. The hard workouts in the Texas heat, two-a-day practices, bootcamps, and only getting a couple water breaks (old school mentality), separated the men from the boys, but furthermore we were pushed beyond the physical and mental limits to understand that we could achieve greatness. Below are a handful of things I learned, most of which are more vital to me today, and will be instilled in my boys as they grow up.

Leadership: The word Leader was spoken over me at an early age by my ninth grade coach, Robby Edwards. He told me that I was different. That I stood out. That I was made for greatness. All 145 lbs. of me believed him, which led me to work even harder. He said that I was not just a leader on the field, but off the field as well with my actions, words, and attitude. He believed in me. He spoke truth over me. Speak truth over your kids! Tell them that they are leaders as it was spoken over me. Tell them that they are destined for greatness. I used to believe that you were either born a leader or you were not. Man was I incorrect. Don't get me wrong, there are some "natural born leaders" out there, but leadership can be learned. And it definitely can be lost if you are not intentional and strive to continue to learn, grow and get better. We need to raise up more leaders. Boys that will become men that will lead their families, lead their neighborhoods and be leaders in the marketplace that embody strong values, integrity, and care for people. Women that are con-fident in themselves, build up others, and aren't afraid to step up for a cause. Being a leader isn't always the easiest job. You have to make hard decisions or go against the status quo. You can't make everyone happy. I like and have to constantly remember Nick Saban, Alabama Head Football coach and seven-time National Champion's quote saying, "If you want to make everyone happy, then go sell ice cream." Being a leader means you stand up for what is right and protect what is weak. Being a leader isn't a sometime activity, it's an all the time activity.

Perseverance: I was a pretty good high school athlete, but more importantly was instinctive on the football field, which made me appear to be faster than I actually was. I knew the game and I knew the opponents play before they ran it due to my studying of the game film and the coaching. I made varsity my sophomore year, which is a big deal in a 5A high school. I played special teams and was destined to start my junior year. Before the start of the season, I got bumped out of my starting safety position and they put a senior, who hadn't thrived as a wide receiver, but was a better athlete in my place. Though he didn't have the defensive mindset and skillset I had, he also had been on varsity since his sophomore year and hadn't become the star player all thought he would. I got moved back to special teams, played some linebacker and was part of the nickel package. Of course, I was mad. I was better. I hit harder; I knew the game better. Were there some politics involved? Maybe. Thankfully my coach Robby and my parents didn't let me sulk very long. They said, it's up to you to decide how to react. You can complain, give up and believe you are a victim. Or you can take this, work harder and believe that you are a victor not a victim. Perseverance is defined as "steadfastness in doing something despite difficulty or delay in achieving success." I chose to grind it out, work even harder and prepare more for my shot. And what happened? I did start my senior year, was nominated team captain, received all district awards, and was granted a recruited walk on position for Baylor University. Today in my business, I persevere daily in a high stress, difficult industry. Nothing is given to me, and life isn't always fair. I celebrate my team's successes but know that it can turn upside in a moment's notice if you don't continue the path. I would not do justice to my boys growing up if I didn't teach them this both verbally and personally in my actions.

Doing the little things correctly: Anyone can do the big things correctly, but doing the little things are what separate good from great. What do I mean here? In football, the little things were the tasks that were not normally noticed but played a huge part in the overall success. Keeping your locker clean, lining up in a straight line, being organized, etc. These are the things that were more of a way of life which embodied discipline. If you could handle these, you would be able to handle the big seeable things correctly, and also be entrusted with more. The Bible speaks to this in Luke 16: 10 when Jesus says, "Whoever can be trusted with very little can also be trusted with much."

Preparation: I alluded to this earlier when I studied the game film and knew the opponent's moves and tendencies, thus allowing me to be a step faster and make big plays. Preparation is key to being successful and gives you a major advantage. In a leadership role, you must stay a step ahead of everyone and always look for opportunities. My mother-in-law has this quote on the side of her fridge, and I believe it wholeheartedly: "Luck is where preparation meets opportunity." Broken down further, luck isn't real, but always be prepared because you never know when a chance might be in front of your face. Preparation has a lot to do with inner drive to do great. Natural ability will only get you so far on and off the field. Preparation is key to success. You must embody this so that your kids learn the value of preparation.

Being Coachable: This might be one of the most underrated but important characteristics of all. I do feel that you either have this or you don't and if you don't, it is most likely because it wasn't instilled in you by your parents. My old defensive back Coach Haag used to say, "You better get nervous if I ever stop coaching you, because that means I don't believe you are coachable anymore." Being coachable is more a model of respect normally to those who are older than you, have experienced more, and have a strong desire to see you succeed. It's sad to see parents today, and when I was growing up, put their kids on a pedestal at an early age. What they didn't know was that they were setting them up for failure then and for the future. Today at 40, I still consider myself coachable. Not always do I like the news delivered to me, but I take it as an opportunity to learn and get better. I urge you to ponder what this means in your kids schooling and athletic endeavors today so you can play a part in shaping them to be coachable.

Attitude: Good or Bad? Positive or Negative? Winning or Losing? Determined or Defeated? Which do you want to be around? Clearly the former of each of these over the latter. Attitude determines the outcome long before the game is over or even begins. If you believe you are going to lose, chances are you have already sealed your destiny. And that is the same in life. Positivity breeds positivity, and negativity breeds negativity. How often have you found yourself around a negative person, and after enough time, your thoughts start shifting to the negative. I've been there. The reverse is even more special. My buddy Bob Borsh lights up a room and when he sees you, makes you feel like the most important person in the building. It's contagious; people gravitate towards him. To advance in life, especially in the negative world we live in, we must raise kids that radiate positivity, determination and a winning attitude.

Teamwork: Football is 100% about teamwork. If 10 people do their job right, and 1 person doesn't, that can mean a broken play, a turnover or even an unnecessary injury. A lot of life is about teamwork. I have a team of 4 in my household. We each depend on each other. I have a team of employees at work. We must be on the same page and all striving for the same goals or we won't get better. I think being a good teammate is similar to being coachable in that a lot of that is instilled by parents at an early age. Are you teaching your kids to be a good teammate? Do they encourage and lift up others in sports or in school? Or are they out for their own interests?

Toughness: Our coaches in high school had a motto: "Teach toughness daily." We also had the bootcamp quote: "Tough times don't last, tough people do." Finally, they instilled in us the difference between "pain" and "injury." Ironically, I used this quote just tonight when taking Kort to swim practice. He scuffed his knee up pretty badly today at school and didn't want to swim because it was burning. I looked at him and asked, "Are you injured or just in pain?" If you are injured, that means you can't continue at all, can barely walk and definitely can't go play with friends. If you are in pain, that means its temporary and it will go away. He wiped his tears, got out of the car, and had a fantastic swim practice. Look, life is tough. Are we going to raise up kids that talk themselves out of tough situations, or even worse throw in the towel, or are we going to raise kids that stand firm in tough times and fight through? Mental and physical toughness are so vital in life. And I fully agree that "tough times don't last, but tough people do."

Being on Time: I don't have many pet peeves but being late is one of them. There is no excuse for being late. You can give one, but what it really means is that you didn't care enough to be prepared to get there on time. We were taught Lombardi time growing up in football after the great NFL Hall of Fame Coach Vince Lombardi. The basis of Lombardi time was that to be on time you were to be fifteen minutes early so that you could collect your thoughts and be prepared for your meeting. If you were just "on time," you were late. Teaching your kids to be on time prepares them for life. I can't tell you the number of tough conversations I've had with adults that can't get to a meeting on time. It's embarrassing to them and frustrating to me. Dadvoted reader, instill promptness in your kids! It's an offshoot of respect.

Hard Work: I am thankful that this attribute was instilled in me growing up. I can confidently say and it's no mystery, that nothing is given to you and that you have to work hard to be great. The quote we used during our bootcamps in high school football was, "If it is to be, it is up to me." Now you are probably thinking that I am being contradictive to my teamwork comments above, but I truly believe that you must have the inner desire to get better or you will be stagnant and go backwards. We all know the saying "There is no "I" in team." Okay... but there are a couple of them in initiative, disciplined, motivation, and inspired. There are countless stories of athletes and the 1000's of hours of work dedicated to fine tune their craft. Or of great business leaders that have worked their way from the warehouse to the top of companies. I'm a major proponent of work/life balance so I have to be careful here, but at the end of the day, you are either a hard worker or you are not. We need more kids to grow up to be people that work hard. That's how we were wired. Lazy or even worse, entitled people, are not going to succeed. We can go toe to toe on labeling a generation like we have done with millennials or blaming technology, but at the end of the day, we have to be present and proactive in teaching our kids to suck it up and work hard. Bottom line.

Accountability: I lean towards integrity when I think of accountability. That is doing the right thing even when no one is looking. Accountability and keeping yourself accountable means that you are going to do what you say, when you say you are going to do it. Period. It's the high standard that you have set for yourself to make you and the people around you better. It's the responsibility to account for your actions. We live in a world of victims, of people who think everything and everyone is out to get them. You have to take ownership when things aren't going your way or when you mess up and uncover what you yourself can do to improve the situation. You can't control others. Don't let your kids grow up to be victims. As the leader of a business, victims suck most of the life out of me. Don't be one, don't raise one!

Self-Evaluation: After every game, we would watch the film as a team. If we were victorious the night before, this was a pleasant experience. If defeated, it was a nightmare. Either way, this time was used to evaluate the team and individual play. We would watch each play numerous times to celebrate the good and uncover the bad. The bad was sometimes flat out embarrassing but was used as a teaching moment to help us get better. Our head football coach would often say, "the big eye in the sky don't lie," when referring to watching the game or practice film. After finishing up my disappointing junior year that I spoke of earlier, I had to self-evaluate if there was anything I did wrong that hindered my chances that year. I remembered coming into camp ten or so pounds overweight and my endurance was lacking. I wasn't going to let that happen again and took steps to join a summer workout program which led me to going into camp my senior year in the best shape I'd ever been in. Lots of times we hide from self-evaluation as we don't want to expose our weaknesses or short comings. I now look at this as a way to get better. With my boys, we do a self-check every six months or so usually during a holiday break and then after summer break. I ask questions like; what do you think you could improve on? And is there anything you should be doing less of? I usually know the answers to these questions, but it's good to see them think and talk through it. It's good to reset and have a discussion to help them get back on track where needed. Look, at 40, I need a reset more than I want to admit. There are often times when I get off track, need to redirect my motives and realign my thoughts and actions. Self-evaluation is necessary to growth.

Goal Setting: Do you set goals? Are you writing them down? Are they posted somewhere that you see them daily? We've all heard it time and again about the importance of goal setting. But setting the goal might be the easiest part. Its creating and executing the plan that is the make or break of it coming to fruition. Showing up daily to achieve those goals is where the rubber meets the road. Setting checkpoints for your goals and celebrating milestones keeps you on track and not burned out. Accepting setbacks as learning opportunities keeps you centered and allows for you to realign where needed. Allow for yourself and for your kids to dream big! Create that culture in your household. Our bootcamp quote was, "Shoot for the moon, the worst thing that could happen is that you fall amongst the stars." What great perspective! What a great mindset to have. God has big plans for your life. Bigger than you could ever conjure up in your own mind. But you are different. You have the mind of Christ (1 Corinthians 2:16). Ask for God to put big dreams in your heart, uncover what that is, write it down, and go after it!

Winning: Winning wasn't something that was taught; it was expected. We all want to win and be winners. Especially when the work you've put in merits victory. Being on top is great! But sustaining it is hard. People are vying for that spot. At times you have to re-create, re-invent and possible re-purpose yourself to stay on top. I think of Tiger Woods changing his golf swing at the peak of his career as he knew that his current swing wouldn't hold up and was too taxing on him. I guess the bigger question is how do you win? Do you win with grace and give credit to those around you? Or are you patting your own back with the hand that's not holding the trophy? That's a scary place to be. Moreover, what are you teaching your kids? That winning is everything? Or, that if they work hard, and be a good teammate the rest will fall into place? I see some kids in the sports we play that I want to dropkick across the court because they already exude arrogance, self-centeredness, and cockiness. But I do contain myself and realize quickly that this is being taught and accepted by their parents.

Losing: Losing sucks. I hate losing more than I love winning, but, it's a part of life. It can bring out the best or the worst in people. Are you a sore loser? Or do you take defeat in stride knowing that you gave your all and left it all out on the field? Now if you didn't work your hardest, prepare like crazy and execute, you deserve to lose. Teach your kids about losing. Sometimes you are just outmanned. Sometimes you are outcoached or outhustled or heaven forbid the referee took over. Take losing as a learning opportunity. If you don't like it, then change something. Maybe something drastic, or maybe it's subtle. That goes back to the self-evaluation piece. Walk with your kids in defeat. Be empathic out the gate. Encourage often through the losses. Give a few hours (even a full day) before you try and step in and fix.

Grit: "Grit is a personality trait possessed by individuals who demonstrate passion and perseverance towards a goal despite being confronted by significant obstacles and distractions. Those who possess grit are able to self-regulate and postpone their need for positive reinforcement while working diligently on a task" (*What Is Grit?, n.d.*).[9] All in, grit is the desire to be great regardless of what may be holding you back or getting in your way. IQ and natural ability are important, but not the key factor in determining success like internal conviction, passion, consistency and toughness. I saw this in high school sports. We had some amazing natural born athletes that could pave their own way through college and even into the professional ranks but didn't have the intestinal fortitude to make it happen. It was sad but happened often. Our coaches had a saying for these athletes that looked the part but couldn't play the part. They would say, "Looks like Tarzan, plays like Jane." In my current role, I made a huge revenue statement and goal in my first weeks on the job and knew it was a reachable goal. Seven years later, we are just now reaching this goal and let me tell you, it was obtained with numerous setbacks and challenges. But we kept our head down and focused through all of it. Talk to your kids about grit. Have grit in your marriage to ensure that your marriage doesn't become part of the divorce statistic. Have grit in raising your kids that no matter what they do you continue to love them, pray over them and guide them. Be consistent, face obstacles head on and be diligent.

Never give up: I was taught if you ever start quitting, it will become easier and easier. I've seen it in many people. When times get tough, they walk away. They change their scenery when they can't change their circumstance. Just to have the cycle start all over again a couple years later. They quit their marriage when it doesn't go their way. They don't get a promotion, so they move on. They pick up their toys and go home. Look, there are times you have to pack it up and move on. But it can become habitual in nature. Life is tough. It isn't fair. Nothing just falls in your lap. You got to go get it. Sustain under heat and pressure. That is how diamonds are created. Don't let your kids quit. If you commit to a sport, see it through to the end of the season. No matter what. Don't let them take the easy way out. It will follow them in life.

Life is more important than sport: Our coaches wanted us to be bigger winners off the field than on the field. To be men of courage and faith in the classroom and at home. Athletics was fun, but it was short term. There was always going to be the last play for all of us. What was most important was taking what we learned and applying it to life. To live with integrity, to care about people from all walks of life, and to strive for greatness in all things.

Our head coach had a quote he'd leave us with before a long weekend that has stuck with me for all this time; "Don't do anything to embarrass yourself, your family, or the Temple Wildcats" (Coach Bob McQueen). Dadvoted reader, I hope you exemplify these characteristics above whether you were a four-year starter, or the water boy; whether you played football or were on the yearbook committee. I'm thankful that these were taught to me through sport, not for the moment, but for a lifetime. Your duty as a dad is to guide your kids through these traits so they can better serve and furthermore thrive in life.

SLEEP, EXERCISE, & NUTRITION

To ACHIEVE ULTIMATE Dadvoted status (yes, this is real), you must maintain consistent habits over a long period of time. You must be a fine-tuned, well-oiled machine to be able to take on the punches of life head on and still have energy to raise your kids passionately. To accomplish this, you must up your game in how you take care of yourself. I'm not saying you have to shred the Dad Bod, which is almost impossible to do while being a selfless person, but that's not the point here. The main point is for you to be able to ooze excitement and passion for raising your kids, out serve your wife, and thrive at work, you must take care of yourself. Sleep, exercise and nutrition are the key foundations to keeping you fueled so that you can encourage and operate at your highest level possible. Sluggish people don't inspire. Lethargic leadership doesn't exist. Exhausted encouraging doesn't make an impact. You have to take care of yourself. This all looks different for whatever stage of life you are in, but I am proud to admit that I am in better shape at 40 than I was at 30. I know men in their 50's that are ripped. I've had leaders in their 70's still running circles around guys in their 50's. I speak a lot to the present, but what you do or don't do today will affect you later in life. Let's be nimble, let's be strong, let's be fresh. I'm not anywhere close to thinking or writing about being Grand-dadvoted, but let's live correctly today, taking care of ourselves properly, so that we can encourage, inspire and further our legacies when we are grandfathers.

If you have yourself in line, it will be much easier for this to be passed onto your kids. Other than training your kids up spiritually, I think one of the most important things you can teach them is how to properly take care of themselves. I'm not just talking about hygiene; I'm talking about establishing lifelong patterns that will help them excel in all aspects of their life. To help their mind, body and soul be fueled and work at its peak. To give them clarity. To give them a foundation to feel good and to take control of their immunity. It all starts and ends with sleep, exercise, and nutrition. Before I go any further, I will note that I'm not a registered physician, dietitian, or nutritionist. But I am aware of what it takes to feel good, and I also see a lot of parents turning a blind eye to their kid's overall well-being by not establishing ground rules for their family's overall health.

Sleep – There is nothing much better than a complete night's sleep. Thankfully we have had really good sleepers from early on. I fully believe it is because we (mainly Keeli) put them on a schedule early. Now as they are growing up, we still have them on a consistent schedule, even on weekends. We do tend to get laxer in the summer, but we do not allow our boys to stay up to the wee hours. We also don't let them stare at devices after 8 pm (actually, we don't allow them on tablets during the week, except for 30 minutes after school). The bright light in the tablets sensors your eyes to wake up and then can cause you trouble falling asleep. Teaching your kids good sleep habits early on will add to their success and productivity in college and as young professionals. Sleep is key for the body to function, stay healthy and grow. I urge you to please take sleep seriously for your kid's sake.

Exercise – Look, I'm not telling you that you need to put your kids on a strict exercise regimen. All I recommend is that they are active. And you as a parent play a part in that as well. Do you go outside with your kids? Are you active with them? Do you go on bike rides with them? We bought a trampoline about 6 years ago and I still jump with the boys. I mainly do it because I get a chance to play and connect with them. But deep down, I also know that 15 minutes on the trampoline is a pretty good workout. Though Keeli and I are not the complete model of health and wellness, our boys see us exercising every week in the house and I hope those good habits rub off through osmosis on them. Exercise is also a great stress reliever and when we exercise, we tend to eat better and sleep better (bullseye!).

Nutrition – How your kids fuel their bodies is a key determining factor in how they perform in school, in sports and impacts their overall immunity and health. I believe that it is important to begin talking about food and nutrition as early as you can and minimizing the amount of sugar and processed foods your kids eat. I'll also be the first to tell you that we are not perfect by any means. We keep frozen chicken tenders on hand, have a candy jar and we eat pizza almost every Friday night. I can also say that for the most part, we have not had extremely picky eaters, though Keeli may disagree. Many parents struggle in this department due to stubborn kids, convenience or are just plain whooped after a long day. Small steps in your family's health will shape them for the rest of their lives. A few tips include:

- Do not have soda available in your house and minimize sports drinks and other sugary drinks –We allow them here and there, but it is not something that is easy to grab here.

- Blend smoothies for your kids – You can hide really good veggies in a fruit smoothy, like spinach, for example, and your kids will never know. Keeli actually blends spinach with a small amount of water and makes spinach ice cubes that she throws in the blender as ice. They boys never know that they are eating spinach.
- Talk about portion control and how food gives them energy
- Meal prep on weekends
- We take Juice Plus tablets and the kids take the gummies to make sure we get close to consuming all the fruits and vegetables we need to stay healthy.

The CDC states on their website that 20.7% of kids between the ages of six and eleven and 22.2% of 12-to-19-year olds are considered obese.[10] This is a very disturbing statistic that I believe can be reversed with good habits of sleep, exercise and nutrition that are engrained at home from an early age. Small steps taken today in these three areas of life today will pay dividends for your kid's overall physical and mental health today and in the future. Please eliminate all the excuses of time, energy or financial burdens when it comes to your kid's health. There is a way to execute this if your priorities are balanced and you have a plan. Being Dadvoted means that you do what it takes to ensure your kids live healthy, and have healthy habits and lifestyles seen and shown to them.

THE TALK

THE DAUNTING SEX talk. What do you say, what do you not say? When do you have it? Can you avoid it? Absolutely not! Let me first say that I remember my mom telling me to "keep my pecker in my pants," and that was the crux of the sex talk from my parents. I will say this again and again, as a parent you must be aware of what is happening in your kids' lives. You want to control the narrative, especially up-front vs having to un-explain what some kid on the playground said. Though a kid may be the same age by the number of years they have lived, they are not the same age when it comes to maturity. For example, I had the full sex talk with Keaton when he was nine years old. Kort is nine years old right now, and he is nowhere near ready to have the same full talk that Keaton and I had a couple years ago. Also, if a nine-year-old has a 15-year-old brother at your kids' elementary school, I guarantee he knows more than he should know over the nine-year-old that is the oldest in his household.

Before I share my personal experience with the sex talk, let me start by saying you must take baby steps when explaining sex and you can't go right into "let me tell you what me and mommy did to make you." Nature is a great place to start. Plants and animals are things young kids are excited about. We started by talking about how plants and animals have seeds and how they must be fertilized to grow. That then led to talking about males and females and how we have different body parts and how God created us differently and that dads have a seed that they give to the mom to create babies, etc. Of course, these talks didn't happen all in one sitting, but over time as things came up. Keaton has always been curious and would ask more questions. I remember us being outside and two dragonflies were stuck together, and he asked, "what are they doing." I started to freak out, but I calmly said, they are making a baby. I asked him if he had any other questions and he said "no," and went about his way. At an even earlier age, Keaton drew a picture of everything he saw at the farm from the weekend, when we had taken him to Papa Alan's farm. And he created this gem of a picture:

Yes, this picture is a classic, and will probably be distributed at his wedding one day. But as you can see, he was curious and asking lots of questions. This all came to head when we were watching a show on Netflix called Absurd Planet. This was a series of episodes that talked about really unique things in nature with a narrator that said funny and off the wall comments throughout the show. We were watching one night with Keaton and the show was all about animal procreation. Of course, there were tons of sexual jokes, some subtle and some not so much, but it was all in all appropriate and funny as all get out. The segment that made the lightbulb go off that he was ready for the talk was when he saw two deer mounted up and he asked me if that was how me and mommy made babies. As most guys would, I had a comeback in my mind that wasn't appropriate, but I held back, and I think I stalled and changed the subject. Immediately after, Keeli told me to have the talk with him as soon as possible.

I know many dads who like to take their sons on a guy's trip to have this conversation, and I like that idea and still might do it with Kort one day, but first of all, I'm not a camper and second, I felt like this talk needed to happen quickly. So, I decided to take him on a "man date." We went out to dinner, and I opted out of the kid's menu telling him that he was a big boy and we were ordering off the big boy menu.

We chatted casually during dinner, and I ordered one big stout beer to get my liquid courage up. After dinner, I told him I wanted to have a serious chat with him, and he perked up. I asked him if he had ever heard the word sex before. He said, "yes, like in Bruno Mars song he says, "sex by the fire at night." That threw me way off guard, but I kept it together (also another pointer of how your kids learn about things through music and pop culture). Either way, I then asked him if he knew what that meant and he said, "is that how babies are made?" I said yes. He then asked me how the father gave the seed to the mommy. I reminded him that God made men and women with different parts and that once they get married, they "come together" to have a baby. He then looked at me again and said, "so how does the seed get from you to her?" I took a deep breath and went for it. I said that daddy carries the seed in his testicles and to get the seed from him to her he has to put his penis inside her vagina. His face was in shock.

I then brought this back to God's plan and said that God's plan is for a man and a woman to get married first before they do this. I also told him that some people do this when they are not married and that doesn't make them bad, nor do we condemn or judge them, but that we try our best to follow God's plan in everything.

But he had more questions. "So...is this like a special moment with you and mom?" I said yes, this is also a way for a married couple to connect with each other and it's a gift from God. "So... do you lock the door and shut the windows?" Yes, this is a private moment between two people. He said, "I can imagine so because sex by the fire at night sounds dangerous." I said, it can be (thank you Bruno). Finally, in reference to the absurd planet episode when the deer are mounted up, "does mom ever say, Oh Dear." I wanted to say not enough, but at that point I ordered dessert and asked for the check.

This is a classic story that I experienced but was so thankful that I was able to control the narrative and present God's plan for marriage and sex. I also made sure to tell him that this was a private conversation between me and him (and mommy) and that he wasn't supposed to go to school and tell all his friends what he learned and certainly not to tell his younger brother. All in, if you are open with your kids at an early age, these conversations are awkward, but not miserable. They just want to know the truth. I will admit though that I prepared for this with Keeli, and I prayed a lot as well.

THE EARLY BIRD
GETS THE WORM

WHAT COSTS NOTHING, is always running at the same speed, and we are all given the same amount of it each day? Time that is. Time is our most valuable resource yet doesn't always get the attention that is needed. We are always up against it and wish we had more of it. We feel that we never have enough and are often saying "where on earth did the time go." I would like to spend some "time" today talking about time and hopefully shed some new light to help us navigate better.

First, I would like to let you in on a secret way for you to add a full month to your year. Hopefully that perked your interest and no this is not a gimmick. If you are currently getting up at 6:30 am, which I feel is standard for most non-commuting folks, and you adjust that to 5:00 am for a year, you now have 547.5 hours of more time. Divide that by 16 for the number of hours per day that you are awake and you just added 34.2 days to your year. Just think what that can do on so many levels to ease your anxiety and help you feel that you aren't always behind. Even just adjusting the time you wake up by an hour would add almost 23 more <u>full</u> days to your year. I hope you see that as liberating. And it is doable!

Now let's talk about the current usage of hours that you are awake. Based on statistca.com, the average American spends over three hours each day watching TV alone and just over two hours per day on social media platforms! This is very staggering and adds to the "always running behind" that I mentioned above. Some of this may seem drastic, but please take it for what it's worth. You may already be in the habit of getting up early with little to no TV and/ or social media time, and I applaud you big time. I guess my question for you would be, how are you spending that additional time? If it's just career and work related, I would like to challenge you to reevaluate this additional time to make sure that you are using it to personally better yourself mentally, spiritually, physically, and emotionally. May I suggest the following:

Quiet time – Maybe I should retitle this entry as; "The Early Bird Gets in the Word." Meeting with Jesus is my richest time in the morning. It sets the tone for my day. I do a devotional, read scripture, pray over it and for my day. If you do this day after day, week after week, month after month, it will grow to be something you can't live without. It also rejuvenates your soul in so many ways that you can't even put into words. Trust me on this!

Exercising – 30 minutes per day. Get in, get out. No need for a fancy gym that takes you 30-40 minutes round trip to commute to, unless it works as part of your work routine. There are so many apps and at home streaming workouts you can do. Exercising reduces stress, increases confidence and overall makes you feel good. I don't have to tell you this. Just do it!

Reading/Learning – What skill do you want to learn? Is there a language you want to learn so you can then travel to that country? Do you want to be a better parent? Leader? Employee? Reading is so key to continual development. This is coming from someone who refused to read for many years. I now have stacks of books I am reading with a goal to read one book per month. My theory is that you are either growing or going backwards. There is no in between. Let's choose growth over stagnation. Set a goal, stick to it!

Journaling – I understand that very few of us are writers or aspire to be. What if you decided to buy a Bible and journal letters to your kids in the margins? I started this over a year ago when I got the idea from Mark Batterson's book *Praying Circles around your Children*. What a rich and meaningful gift that will be given to each of my boys one day that will stay in their lives forever. They will have my view and perspective on God's Word forever. They will see my journey with Jesus through all seasons of life and be challenged to seek Jesus in the same manner. Also, I recommend journaling in general on life. I reference journaling in the prelude of this book. Though I only wrote here and there before starting my writing journey, it is so cool to see God's hand in my life through major life changing events or when I thought there was little hope. Leaving behind your words is something that is often not done and taken for granted. What a gift to give back to your family. Write something down!

Dadvoted reader, time management is so key. If you want to take back over your life, it starts with you and your schedule. Yes, sleep is key and vital to your success. The combination of when you get up and what you do when you get up determines if you are going to thrive or just survive. Give the first part of your day to God, exercise consistently, read or learn something new, and journal your progress and life situations. You will be more mentally aware to attack the workday and won't be such a ball of stress. Do this for yourself and for your family. This type of attacking the day mentality is contagious. Your spouse will be encouraged, and your kids will see what you do more through your actions and reactions if the tone for your day is set correctly. The choice is yours!

PRESSURE COOKER

THE PRESSURE TO perform is surmounting. Perform at work, provide at home, set up our people for success. That's ok, we are grown men. We expect this. A lot of us elevate our game when our back is against the wall and the pressure is high. High heat and high pressure create diamonds. Most of us are up for the challenge. What pressure though are we transferring to our kids? I talk a lot about instilling greatness in your kids and speaking leadership traits over them, but at what cost? Are you coming from a place of love or a place of selfishness? Are you a driver? Are you placing heat and pressure on your youngster to perform today at the highest level possible all for what you think is for his/her greater good? We know the stories of high performing athletes whose dad drove them to greatness, i.e., Tiger Woods. Is this the only way? To have your thumb on your kid so firm at an early age because you "know what's best for them?" I'm assuming there are probably a lot more resentment and burnout stories that never get published or talked about.

Raise your hand if you've seen the psycho parent at the youth basketball game or swim meet wearing their eight-year-old out about their performance? Now raise your hand if that's you. There is always a right and wrong way to address things and unfortunately, we dads (me included), tend to go for the firm, emotional response. At the end of the day, we can talk and should talk about inner drive, but we can't force it. We can try, but if it's reinforced with negativity, what do you think the response is going to be? Your child either wants it and will put in the time, or they don't. There is nothing wrong with that. I laugh, as I recently watched a dad giving the pregame speech to a handful of peewee baseball players on YouTube and he said, "If your dad told you to come out here and have fun regardless of if you win or lose, then he is a loser! We are here to win and only win." Pretty funny stuff, and I do like his candor though this probably turned a lot of parents off. Winning is fun and is expected in life, but you are raising kids. Your goal is to point them in the right direction and guide them, but let them figure out how much effort they want to put into it. If they love something, they will work at it. Yes, we are here to nudge and help them uncover the greatness that they don't see yet, but not to force it. Your kids should try as many sports as they want and play multiple sports while growing up. The forcing them into one sport now and putting all your eggs in that one basket to increase the likelihood of a scholarship is more likely to create burnout.

This isn't just in sports, but also in school. Grades are very important; I'm not going to say they aren't. But is anything less than an A in elementary school unacceptable? What about putting your kids in all AP advanced everything? Know your kids and their strengths. I think we play a part of the problem of all the pressure and stress that is being put on our kids at such an early age. The goal is to have well-rounded kids, not robots. The more pressure you put on them to succeed early the chances are that they can burnout and suffer from anxiety and depression.

Ephesians 6:4 says, "Fathers, do not exasperate your children; instead, bring them up in the training and instruction of the Lord." Exasperate means to irritate or frustrate intensely. If you are always in their ear, wanting them to be better, and pushing them way too hard, you are going to frustrate them. Look, I'm not saying that we need to be soft here, but I am inferring that we need to let our kids be kids when they are young. Plant seeds of hard work, perseverance, and doing the right thing early and often, but not in a dictator, "my way or the highway," format. When they are lazy or don't prepare for something and they fail, calmly walk them through what went down, why they failed, and ask them if they did everything in their power to succeed. Cool heads always prevail. How do you like your boss to come at you? From a driver, dictator, one sided point of view, or from a coaching, calm perspective?

Dadvoted reader, let your kids be kids. They are going to have plenty of time to be in the pressure cooker of life. The Bible says to bring them up in the training and instruction of the Lord. When I have God in the center of my life, and am seeking and living for Him, the pressure seems to ease off me. I let go and let God. I don't worry, I don't stress, I don't feel the burnout and run ragged. So, let's follow suit and train our kids up in the instruction of the Lord so the pressure cooker of life can be unplugged on them. Not that they won't have the stress, but they will be equipped to handle it.

TRASH IN, TRASH OUT

I **HAD A** friend in high school whose family mantra was "Trash in, Trash out." What did they mean by this? Basically, what you consume will imprint in your mind, take root in your heart, will be manifested in your thoughts and is likely to flow out of your mouth and in your actions. They applied this to everything from TV shows, movies, music and the people they associated with as friends. And this was in the late 90's, long before we had the internet and the world always attached to us via a cell phone. Social media didn't exist. "TikTok" referred to a clock sound, and was not a rabbit hole to wander down for hours at a time. How much more should we all adopt this same mantra today to protect and guide our kids? Our kids don't even need to know how to spell something risqué to search for it, but just have to speak it into a smart device. Scary stuff.

Dadvoted reader, I urge you today to check in and challenge any areas where you have been lackadaisical for both your kids and for yourself. It's easy when your kids are young to set firm boundaries on what they watch but over time you can get complacent. Let me tell you, the companies building apps and advertising don't care about the well-being of your child. That app that you approved six months ago and thought was appropriate for your youngster, has had multiple updates and adjustments. Parental restrictions are good, but kids today are smarter than you can imagine. They already know how to clean their internet searches, delete the deleted files and even bypass and reset the parental guidelines. These are standard tricks and workarounds. Don't be naïve. I know your kids are "angels," but they are curious. Their friends may have older siblings that are exposing their siblings to inappropriate things that in turn are being brought to your elementary school. My goal here is to increase awareness and not increase your desire to move to the remote wilderness. As good as that sounds, your kids are going to be exposed to things at an age that you don't want them to be, no matter how hard you try. The "F" word is already plastered all over our elementary playground here in Bible belt suburbia. We are getting questions about words and sexual acts at an age way before I ever knew these things existed.

Ok, now that I got your heart rate up and you are probably texting your wife to talk about the internet restrictions you may or may not have in place, let's get back to YOUR home. What are you allowing to be watched in your house? I'm not going to make a specific list for you. Some may think that The Simpsons is appropriate for elementary school kids, some may not. To each his own. I'm not here to debate, but I will tell you what some of the boundaries are that we've put in place at the stage of life we are in with a middle schooler and elementary schooler, most of what we plan to keep in place for a while.

No TVs in the bedroom – We don't keep a TV in our bedroom, so our kids won't get one in their bedroom. As a married couple, we don't keep one in our bedroom as we know that having a TV on can affect your sleep. We choose to read or engage in the art of "talking to each other" at night, which is a lost concept. For our kids, we want them to get good sleep and not to establish a habit of having a TV on when you go to bed. Also, we can't monitor what they watch from the privacy of their bedroom when we are sound asleep.

No cell phone in the bedroom at night – I'm not here to debate when kids should or shouldn't get a cell phone. That depends on the maturity of the kid, the parameters set in place upfront, and the need based on school or after school activities. But our reason for this rule is that we don't need late night curiosity kicking in, or mindless searching taking place. Also, it is not out of the norm for my oldest to wake up to a couple hundred text messages that came through at all hours of the night from kids who don't have cell phone rules in their house.

Movie screening – We carefully screen movies, all movies, even the animated ones. There are a lot of new agendas being presented in kids movies from outlets that were once wholesome in our childhood. I won't say any names but be aware. Same sex attraction, sexual innuendos, gender confusion, disrespecting authority, and body changes can be both subtly and directly portrayed. There are websites that rate these movies and warn of the content, language and borderline scenes. I recommend finding a faith-based site to review these movies.

Talk to your kids often – Be open with your kids. Talk to them. Ask them if anyone has recently said anything that they didn't know what it meant. Ask them if anyone has shown them anything on their phone that was suspect. My youngest has made up his mind not to look at anything that others show on their phone. Tell your kids why we have certain rules and boundaries in place. We say that we want to protect their minds and that Mom and Dad have to also protect their minds even at their age. Talk to them about being exposed to certain things when at other people's houses. If they are simple in nature, don't make them feel bad. Just tell them that it's a show we don't prefer to watch at our house. If it's worse and they are being exposed to something graphic, discuss an exit strategy.

Build trust – Tell your kids to always tell you if they have been exposed to something inappropriate. When they do, don't shame them, ridicule them, or snatch their device away from them in hopes to shelter them. This won't work. This reactionary response will prompt them not to ever bring something back to you that they are curious or concerned about. Stay calm! Level with them. Say things like, "I'm so sorry you were exposed to this." If you don't have the answer right away, tell them this and then set a time to come back and revisit the topic. Don't brush it under the rug.

Pray for you kids and their relationships – We want our kids to be friendly to all, but we also want them to have a core group of solid relationships that encourage each other and challenge each other. This might be one of the most meaningful prayers we can pray. Pray over their friends with them as well; this includes past, present and future friends.

Check your own heart – What are you watching? Are you watching a food video through your Facebook feed that is harmless, but then getting sucked into the following video that is inappropriate? It starts simple and then snowballs. I just removed all videos from my Facebook feed for that reason. A video on skateboarding fails, is followed up by a video of a lady in a low-cut dress, and so on and so forth. Protect your heart and mind.

Set adult boundaries – What? But I'm an adult? I can do what I want. Well, your kids are sponges. "Do as I say, not as I do" isn't the model we want to portray. It confuses your kids. It drives their curiosity even more. Keeli and I have decided that we are not going to watch rated R movies. I know you are going to think we are crazy, but we only watched three episodes of *Yellowstone* before I decided that this wasn't good for me. That's right, I made the decision. One of the first episodes had Beth fully naked in cow trough (classy right?). She got out and walked back to the house. That vision is now ingrained in my mind. I'm a guy, I think God's creation of woman is some of his most masterful work ever. But He also gave me a beautiful wife who I should only have eyes for. I don't need to have other visions of naked women in my mind. It's not healthy.

Language boundaries–Keeli has a three "F" bomb limit on anything we watch. Unfortunately, that is starting to eliminate us even watching PG13 movies. Funny story on this: she was once on a plane traveling for business and some jackleg business guy sitting next to her was spitting bombs all over the place and being extremely obnoxious. She said, "excuse me sir, but I have a three "F" bomb limit and you have already well exceeded it." He looked at her and shockingly said, "Who are you? One of those Jesus lovers?" She responded with "that's exactly who I am." That a girl!! Here's the thing about language that confirms this whole entry. I know from experience if I watch something with lots of bad language or I'm around a group of guys that speak not only ill of people, but also use colorful language often, I start to think those words in my head. I may not use them, but they have rooted in my heart and are in my thoughts. Even as adults, we need to continually monitor ourselves, who we associate with, and what we expose ourselves to.

Be prepared – You can't be prepared to answer every question that comes your way. That's expected and okay. But you can prepare your mind and your heart. There are so many resources on parenting out there via reading and podcasts. Instead of listening to sports talk radio on your commute, maybe try listening to a book on how to talk to your kids or listen to a podcast on real issues your children are experiencing these days. One recommendation is Mandy Majors with *NextTalk*. She has two books and a podcast that speaks to a lot of this, that I have found to be extremely helpful at a minimum helping me with my initial response.

Dadvoted reader, let's set the tone for our household with all media. Re-establish boundaries where needed and have real conversations with our kids. Today is the day we take the trash out!

"MONEY MONEY MONEY MONEY"

ARE YOU SINGING the song in your head? "For The Love of Money" was recorded by the The O'Jays in the 70's, but many of us know the song from the show *The Apprentice*. The topic of money is important as there tends to be such a skewed view about its purpose. There is also so much to teach our kids about money which will impact how they view it as they grow up. Making it, saving it, spending it, giving it, budgeting it, investing it, the good side of it and the ugly side of it. Making money at its core is not a bad thing. It's the consuming nature and love of money that can overtake us. The bible doesn't shy away from discussing it.

> "Those who want to get rich fall into temptation and a trap and into many foolish and harmful desires that plunge people into ruin and destruction. For the love of money is the root of all kinds of evil. Some people, eager for money, have wandered from the faith and pierced themselves with many griefs" (1 Timothy 6:9-10).

Maybe you were taught strict habits about respecting the money you brought in and how you spend it. Maybe you lived in a family that spent it before you had it. Maybe you fall into the far side of one of these methods yet married someone who falls into the complete opposite side. Not only has that probably caused some tension but hopefully you've made adjustments to meet in the middle. If not, you probably have a constant battle at hand in your household. If you are on the same "healthy" page with your spouse in terms of money, I applaud big time! Your next responsibility is to teach money management to your kids.

Do you talk about money with your kids? Do you give them an allowance for the chores they do? Do you talk about saving and spending wisely with them? What about tithing? This is such a good place to discuss the role that money serves, God's blessings and provisions, as well as being a good steward of the gifts given to us. However, being real here, I have two boys with two polar opposite views on money. Keaton, my oldest, if given $1 million would give 95% of it to church and help people. He's an old soul and I love his heart for people and for good causes. Kort, on the other hand, would spend 150% of it on toys, candy and adventures, before he even got it and before the taxes were taken out. I love his heart for thrill seeking and having fun. So, we have got a lot of work to do here over the next six and eight years before these crazy people leave our house.

What about you? Do you talk to your wife about your expenses? Do you have a budget? Do you actually stick to it? Are you in debt? Are you concerned about your future as it relates to your finances? These are real questions and questions you can't shy away from. I understand that we are in different places and stages in life. That life can hit us hard in many ways. But I also know that we as men tend to brush some things under the rug and just grit through in hopes of better days. I do know this about Jesus as well. He wants us to live in freedom—all kinds of freedom—especially financial freedom. This doesn't mean that you are going to have millions of dollars and all kinds of money stockpiled. But I do know that He doesn't want you to be burdened by debt which adds stress and strips joy out of your life. What consumes you? Is there anything else acting as lord in your life? Does money consume your thoughts? Today's money, tomorrow's money, etc.? Yes, you must be aware and prepared, but you can't be dependent and driven by only money. The Bible talks about the uncertainty of wealth.

> "Command those who are rich in the present world not to be arrogant nor to put their hope in wealth, which is so uncertain, but put their hope in God, who richly provides us with everything for our enjoyment" (1 Timothy 6:17).

What are you rich in?

- Money or morals?
- Spending or serving?
- Wealth or overall health?
- Getting or giving?
- Bringing home the bacon or bringing home balance?
- Hundies or helping?
- Having a lot of paper or a lot of peace?
- Dinero or deeds?
- Loot or love?
- Making moola or making disciples?
- Greed or God?

Dadvoted reader, it's all about your priorities and your heart. Who are you serving? Jesus states it the best when he says, "No one can serve two masters. Either you will hate the one and love the other, or you will be devoted to the one and despise the other. You cannot serve both God and money" (Matthew 6:24).

I challenge you today regardless of whatever stage of life you are in with money. If you have plenty, that you are convicted to give more, to live simpler and help others. If you are struggling, that you would examine everything you are doing or not doing to help dig out. God needs us to be financially healthy so that our heart and mind can focus on the tasks and calling He has for our lives. The enemy wants to keep us trapped. Seek help and seek the Lord. There are so many resources, but it starts with you making the decision.

PORN

Lord, I need You to show up as I talk about this most agonizing topic. I have held off long enough knowing that there would be a battle here. Protect my mind, heart and soul as I research this and write. Surround Your angels around me that I won't wander or be tempted beyond what I can handle. Keep the enemy away from me. So many men struggle here secretly. This is affecting marriages and mental health and they don't recognize it. Kids are being exposed and getting the wrong information about what You deemed as beautiful between a husband and wife. May my words be Your words. To convict and not condemn, to inspire not create isolation, to give hope and healing. Too many dads are in bondage. We need them released. By Your Spirit and Your blood move in this moment over this topic.

EVERYTHING AROUND US has been overly sexualized. Everything around us has been digitalized as well. We have access to just about anything we want to see in our back pocket. This combination of convenience linked with curiosity is allowing our kids to be exposed to bad things at a very early age. A study from the British Board of Film Classification (2020) says that most kids today are exposed to porn by age 13. I'll admit that I still remember my first exposure in middle school. My best friend and I had to sneak into his neighbor's garage and grab a magazine that we knew was stashed. I also had a fuzzy channel that I could barely make out some nudity of soft-core porn, which basically left my mind and imagination to uncover as I couldn't see much. Porn was hard to get. We had no access to movies and couldn't buy magazines. Man, has it changed. Today, it's in high-res 5k with the click of a few buttons. All positions, all ages, all genres. The world is your oyster. Your six-year-old can ask Siri to show "naked women" or "boobs" and if your restrictions aren't in place, you've allowed your six-year-old to see whatever pops up. They are already seasoned on clicking through links and videos on the daily and can now be exposed to the worst of the worst right in your home within moments. Are you having any conversations with your kids yet? Or just hoping for the best? I urge you to get with your wife and begin creating a plan immediately. We started with our kids years ago by reading them the book *Good Pictures Bad Pictures*, by Kristen A Jenson to raise awareness that there are inappropriate things online and to begin planting seeds. We have started having different conversations with our middle schooler now as a lot of kids have phones at school. We turned his air drop off as sending nudes is already taking place, yes, in middle school! Dads, we must be aware and intentional. We can't skirt around the fact that the world is trying to pollute our kids minds as early as possible. Also don't just think that this is a problem for boys. More and more girls are being exposed to porn. Some out of curiosity, to learn about how to have sex, or because it is forced on them. Don't think just because you have daughters, you get a hall pass from this difficult conversation.

Shifting to Dads, I have a straight question here. Are you watching any sort of porn? This isn't just a question for nonbelievers of Jesus. I say this as approximately 91.5% of men and 60.2% of women report consuming porn in the past month, according to a 2020 study (Solano, Ingrid; Eaton, Nicholas R.; and O'Leary K. Daniel – 2020 in Journal of Sex Research). Are you crossing the line anywhere viewing inappropriate material? Have you found a way to justify it in your mind (well, it's just soft core, or it's just pictures, not videos)? Are you stuck in a rut, or in a pattern you can't get out of? Just like the effects of alcohol or drugs, porn releases dopamine, or that euphoric feeling of pleasure. Once you get some of it, you want more and more. It can become a stronghold and addiction that can lead to mental health issues and relational issues. There is so much linked to it, and I challenge you to research on your own. There is a lot of sex trafficking linked to the porn industry as well. Porn predominately portrays male dominance over women in often violent scenarios. It also is not a real portrayal of sex. Many studies also show that people who regularly view porn have lower relationship satisfaction (www.fightthenewdrug.org).

Dadvoted reader, if you are engaged in any sort of pornographic consumption, you need to STOP! You are not a bad person, nor am I condemning you, but this isn't who you are! This stuff is toxic for your brain, for your marriage and for your mental health. I don't have daughters, but if you do, picture your daughter being objectified. Many of these women are not consenting to sex but are forced into it. This is a hub for trafficking. We've got to stand up and stand firm on this topic. "Flee from sexual immorality!" (1 Corinthians 6:18). "Flee" is not a casual word. It means to take off, run away, escape! I know you aren't going to want to hear this but seek help. Find a recovery group from your church or another church that you don't attend. Line up accountability somehow. You may need to soul search and be real to uncover if you are stuck. Regeneration is another fantastic faith-based recovery program. Check out www.

regenerationrecovery.org. There are over 130 locations across the US and some offering online if you are too far away from a meeting area. You've got to get out of the darkness. Jesus wants to use you for so many things but can't and won't if you continue down this path of blatant sin. Run, Repent, seek Recovery and be Redeemed. You are never too far gone. Jesus says, "I am the light of the world. Whoever follows me will never walk in darkness, but will have the light of life" (John 8:12). Jesus wants you in the light so you can see and walk His path for you.

DEVICE OR VICE?

WE HAVE A new addictive pandemic on our hands. I know using the word pandemic makes a lot of you cringe and I apologize. Over the last 30 years, we have seen the cell phone morph from something only a few had (that was in a bag the size of a shoebox), to now everyone has, and it can even be connected to you via your watch, so you never can lose connectivity. My parents had the mounted cell phone in my mom's fancy black Lincoln Town Car, and she had the strongest plan out there, which included a whopping 30 minutes per month of talk time. Holy smokes we have come a long way! I still remember both my best friend and my neighbor's land line #, yet I don't know my wife or son's cell # today. Can you relate? In college, you would leave for a spring break trip and tell everyone to meet at this place at this time and you know what... we all showed up at that place at that time. Crazy!

First of all, I am not against technology or the advancement of it. Though I'm a late adapter, I have a lot of technology at my disposal and I'm no conspiracy theorist by any means. I do probably only utilize 3% of my phone's capability, but it's necessary to have in order to connect and allow me to do business from just about anywhere, which, for the most part, is a good thing. But we have created a dependency to our phones unlike any other item we have (probably more than power, that is if you have a fully charged phone).

I'm not going to wow you with stats on phone use. We don't need stats to see that there is a societal problem on our hands (or should I say in our hands). Just look around. People are walking down the street on their device. Couples are on a date and are both starring at their phone. Groups of kids are gathered together sitting in a circle and they are all on their phone. The art of the real conversation is crashing in front of us. Is this "smart" phone actually making us smarter? Sure, you have instant access to knowledge and the internet, but are we really growing as humans? I'm not here to answer that question, but when the #1 occupation choice among teens today is to be a social media influencer[11], I think we are going down a tough path for our future.

Kids aren't just the part of this growing problem. Parents are in the throes of it as well. We need to be a better example, so we can also parent the phone better ourselves. Here are a couple questions? When you come home, where does your phone go? When you eat dinner with your family, at home or at a restaurant, is your phone put away or right in front of you. If you are eating dinner as a family together at home (shocker, right) and your phone rings, do you get up from the table to go look at it or answer it? At work, when an employee or co-worker is talking to you and your phone dings or lights up, do you look at it immediately and draw your attention off them to your phone?

Dadvoted reader, you are giving your job a solid 8-10 hours/day if not more. When you get home and your kids are actually at home and not at after school activities or doing homework, you may get an hour or so of time with your family before it is bedtime. Unless you are in a field that is saving people or protecting people, I don't see a need to be attached to your phone after 7 pm. Put it on silent and put it away. Give your kids an hour or so a night of your time to be with them. To talk to them, to play a game with them, to watch a show with them.

Speaking of work, when do you turn your phone off? When do you turn it back on? Do you have a do not disturb feature turned on? Do you work on weekends or whenever your phone dings? Do you actually honor the Sabbath and take a day of rest? Being as connected as we are can be exhausting if you let it. But, here is the good news. You can change this and set new parameters and actually follow them. I know you may think I'm crazy, but I'm not. I run a very intense business that requires a lot of my time, energy and effort, but I have adopted many of the things above. I turn my phone on silent when I get home and I don't answer calls or texts unless it is from family while my boys are still up. I have a do not disturb feature turned on from 10 pm to 7 am (which will change one day when my kids are older and stay out later). I don't start my workday until 7 am, which gives me time to seek Jesus, write and exercise before my phone dominates the rest of my day. I don't work one day a week. It may be Saturday, or it may be Sunday, but I give one of those days to the Lord and am not legalistic about which day I give.

Guys, this all starts at home. The art of the conversation won't die if we continue to have meaningful conversations at home. The being together but not being present will stop if you make it stop. You can put your phone up at a restaurant and have rich convos with your wife, friends and kids. Be the change! Shift the culture!

DISCIPLINE, DISCIPLINING, AND DISCIPLINED

THIS IS A tongue twister for sure. These three "D" words correlate with the three "D" words on the front cover of this book: duty, direction, destiny. Part of manhood is understanding these three words in your own life. But in terms of fathering, it is your duty to teach, direct and live out these 3 "D" words to pass them along to your kids. You teach discipline, you instill disciplining them to correct when your child is out of line or off path, and you live out being disciplined in your own life as a model to your kids. This isn't always pretty, but it's necessary. If you truly care for your kids (which I know you do), you accept this task in your life and don't let it go by the wayside. Let me repeat: this isn't a job for a mom to do by herself.

Discipline – I love the quote by Jocko Willink, former Navy seal, saying, "discipline is greater than motivation." We all have moments where we want change and are motivated to pursue it. Think of the New Year's resolution to start living healthier. That gym is packed those first few weeks of January. Everyone is there to change a habit or behavior. Then reality sets in. You are sore, life is busy, you cherish your sleep. That motivation begins to wean, and you go back to your old ways. I've also seen and experienced those mountain-top moments after a strong church message or men's conference where you walk out ready to conquer the world and live fully for Jesus, just to return back to a state of mediocrity and normalcy (sometimes that very next day). This doesn't make you a bad person, it's hard to stay on track unless you have the mindset shift to that of living a life of discipline. It's about self-control and creating patterns of behavior that seek to stay on track and excel. Your kids must learn this, and it's up to you to train them on this. Talk them through pressing ahead when their motivation is gone to finish the goal, task or mission in front of them. Not to be lazy or give up. Discipline is also a gift from God. 2 Timothy 1:7 says, "For the Spirit God gave us does not make us timid, but gives us power, love and self-discipline."

Disciplining – None of us are a fan of either side of disciplining. Having to correct behaviors by enforcing change to perfect someone's moral character is not something most of us wake up early looking forward to do. I've met a few in the work force and they either were picked on as a kid, picked last at recess, or had an overbearing father. Either way, disciplining is a part of life and to our kids it should come from a place of love, and not something we love to do.

Scripture points to God disciplining us:

> "Know that in your heart that as a man disciplines his son, so the Lord your God disciplines you." Deuteronomy 8:5

> The Word also says that those who the Lord is disciplining are blessed. Job 5:17 And that the Lord disciplines those He loves. Proverbs 3:12

And for parenting, Proverbs 23:13 says, "Do not withhold discipline from a child; if you punish them with the rod, they will not die. Punish them with the rod and save them from death."

So, there's your permission to spank! Straight from the Word of God. All joking aside, Dadvoted reader, disciplining your child isn't just an act to correct. It's also an opportunity to instruct. Have a conversation. Keep your cool (I know that's hard in the moment), and love on your kids in a tough moment to redirect their path. God has done that to you and to me. It was never fun, and I'm pretty darn stubborn as well. Be on the same page with your wife on discipling your kids, but you lead.

Disciplined – Or a state of being disciplined. This means you've reached the pinnacle. You are regimented, methodical, and you restrain from what you know isn't good, right or healthy for you. You aren't a robot, but you have the highest standards for yourself and your conduct. You are consistent. Your mindset and mentality *are* unshakable. You can't teach this to your kids, but you can live it out in such a way that it passes on to your kids, and they want it as they see you thrive. My kids know my goals. They also know my big dreams. We talk about them; they see them written down in my office. But more importantly, they see what I'm doing to make those dreams a reality and that I'm partnering with Christ. I can't fail, I won't fail. I may have setbacks, but those are opportunities to grow and get better.

Dadvoted reader, discipline, disciplining and the state of being disciplined all lead to another "D" word that is the most important part of our duty, direction and destiny and that is creating Disciples. Your ultimate goal as a Father is that your kids would love Jesus and live for Him daily. To believe and follow the ways of Christ with a goal to advance the Kingdom and make Him known. This is why we teach discipline, apply disciplining in love and live a disciplined life.

MARRIAGE MATERIAL

THE DATING SCENE has not started here in the Goodnight household (other than me still dating Keeli), and I'm completely okay with that. I am mentally preparing for this to take place in the future. There are tons of books and thoughts about teenage dating and what it should or shouldn't look like. Though not in the throes of it yet, I must lean on probably the best piece of advice given to me by my mom and that was to never date someone who wasn't "marriage material." That is if they weren't someone that you could see yourself being with forever not to even waste your time. If their values and morals weren't in line with what you know is right and wholesome to not even consider going down the path. Of course, she also said that church was a good place to start. Now for boys, who are more visual in nature, that is normally the last thing on their brains. I recently joked remembering that when I was in 8th grade, I "dated" a 7th grader but told my dad and uncle that she was "built like an 8th grader." What was I even saying? Clearly, I had different priorities and honestly picture it crazy for middle school kids to even be dating (but I guess we did it).

To some you might think or even wonder why a kid in high school would even have the thought of marriage material. I mean, chances are they probably won't get married. Get some practice, don't take it too seriously. I would tend to somewhat agree but would prefer to set the stage for my boys to raise their standards out the gate. Also, to decrease their likelihood of entering into a toxic relationship early on in life. Aligning yourself with someone as a close friend or even more in a dating relationship is a big deal. If the core priorities don't line up, there are increased chances of turmoil. The Bible refers to this spiritually as being yoked. 2 Corinthians 6:14 says, "Do not be yoked together with unbelievers. For what do righteousness and wickedness have in common? Or what fellowship can light have with darkness?"

This verse may be confusing as you would say, "well doesn't Jesus accept all," or "doesn't Jesus hang out with the sinners." The answer to those questions are that you are correct. But being yoked means that you are in a partnership with the other person. Think of two oxen with a yoke (wooden frame) holding them together. They must walk in unison, or there is going to be more strain with it being harder to work and accomplish things. This symmetry is vital in marriage. You are yoked with your wife. You walk step and step together as partners to complete each other and advance. If one is pulling left and the other is pulling right, there is unnecessary strain and frustration. So why would you enter into any relationship that doesn't have the same spiritual foundation. It's done more often than you think. Not only in marriage, but also in business.

So, for my kids, though I don't know all the details and rules at this point in time, my only rule would be to consider dating those that have a spiritual foundation of truth inside of them? I'm not saying that they can't lead a nonbeliever to Jesus, and that we wouldn't be accepting of who they bring home, but I don't think it's wise to pursue deep relationships with someone that doesn't have the same core beliefs rooted inside. I'll gladly accept the hate mail, but I've experienced firsthand the goodness of being yoked with a believer and have witnessed a ton of heartbreak and hurt for those that are unyoked. It's your call how to lead your kids. I challenge you to at least be cognizant. Furthermore, I challenge you today to pray for your kid's future spouse. That they would be yoked and rooted in the things of Christ. It's never too early to begin praying this over them. Hoping for the best isn't a proactive strategy. Partnering in prayer is.

BE A BLAKE

SOMETIMES BECOMING A dad happens immediately upon getting married. You find the love of your life, and she comes with a bundle of joy already attached from a previous marriage or life event. Some call this baggage. Others call this a blessing. You get to decide how you show up for "someone else's kids." It's a big decision and often a deal breaker for men. What if you viewed that as a game changer and not a deal breaker? That's exactly how my buddy Blake approached the situation when he met his bride. He cherished everything about her including the daughter that she brought to the marriage. He humbly accepted the challenge of becoming a dad on day one and it changed him. He realized quickly that it wasn't about him anymore. Not only did marriage do that for him, but a precious little heart and soul of a daughter was now under his care. Some things changed overnight. New responsibilities appeared and his mindset changed. He was already a man's man in a sense, but his heart was softened. He lit up when he talked about his new daughter. He accepted her as part of him immediately. Priorities were realigned, outside influences were brought into check, and he knew it was his time to leave an impact.

We connected early in 2021 to talk about an opportunity to come work for me as my right hand and lead my sales team. We knew each other well but only more or less on the surface. We shared a passion for America's team, that's right the Dallas Cowboys, and at our core were very similar in that we loved people and we loved to have a good time. Though we were there to talk about a major career change, I sensed something different. And not just because of his new responsibilities as a husband and father, but I sensed something else. His faith and love of Jesus was brought up. He had started attending a Bible study and that it was more meaningful and real than ever before. It was a rich conversation. One of the richest I had experienced in our industry to date. An industry where a lot of believers aren't vocal about their love and need for Jesus. An industry that has a lot of people hiding behind who they really are in the name of "fitting in." I remember leaving and calling my wife and saying that I wasn't sure if we were going to become coworkers, but that I could see a mentor/mentee relationship forming.

Blake took his revived passion for Jesus and started meeting with another guy in our industry to encourage each other in their faith and to talk about why so many hide and don't proclaim God's goodness. He and Joey met often, which led them to calling Mat, another industry believer, which led Blake to calling me in early August of 2021. He said, I don't know what this looks like, but I've started a group that wants to become more vocal in our industry to proclaim what Jesus is doing and has done in our lives. That we need to come out of hiding and that there were so many people in our industry that needed to hear this in hopes to become their true selves. We had our first meeting set for mid-August, but it got cancelled. On August 31, Joey called me with the worst news. Blake was killed in a tragic car accident. I was in shock. I called his phone immediately and it was turned off. I couldn't believe this. My heart was crushed. The "why God?" and "why now?" questions flooded my brain. I hurt for his new wife and daughter. I hurt for his amazing mom, who I knew through the industry. This wasn't fair. Why would God take His newest ambassador in our industry so quickly? These are hard questions, and I don't have all the answers but had to press in and remember that God is good and is in control.

Dadvoted reader, there is so much to take in here. First and foremost, I challenge you to be a Blake. I learned so much from him in just over the course of a few months that I want to reflect on. If you have inherited a child for whatever reason, love that child like they are your own. If that child is in your house, they are under your care. Raise that child up with the same love, fervor and passion you would as if they are your own child by blood. Regardless of the relationship with the birth father, you have been put in this child's life by Jesus to point them to Him. Second, if you have a true faith and love for Jesus, proclaim Him. Don't be shy, don't be embarrassed, **be bold**. If you know you are redeemed and are a new creation, tell the world! Not to thump them over the head with a Bible, but to tell them your own story of how who were rescued and made new. No one can ridicule your own story. And we all have a story. Third, live today as if it were your last. Blake embodied that to the fullest. He never met a stranger and always greeted you with a genuine bear hug. Life is way too short. We are consumed with so much that in the grand scheme of things means absolutely nothing. Hug your babies today, cherish your wife a little more, ask for forgiveness where you have done or said some you regret and forgive those that have wronged you. If we could all possess even a small percentage of Blake's qualities, the world would be a better place. Be a Blake!

SECTION 3: CHARGE

ABIDE OR DIE

"RIDE OR DIE" is a phrase I've never heard a guy use. Where I've seen it most often used is between two BFFs celebrating 25-plus years of friendship, who grew up together and are entering into a weekend of hardcore shopping, breaking from being a mom and tooling around a town in the hill country outside of Austin with their "Wine down" matching shirts on. Not really the "gangsta" meaning that it intended to have, but that is how I've seen it used.

So, my goal for us dads seeking ultimate Dadvoted status is that we would create the tagline "abide or die" and get this trending. Are you with me? Urban dictionary is patiently waiting. I see shirts, hats and tatts in the future. Abiding is the act of enduring and continuing for a long time. Jesus states this so eloquently in John 15 when he says, "Abide in me, and I in you. As the branch cannot bear fruit by itself, unless it abides in the vine, neither can you, unless you abide in me. I am the vine; you are the branches. Whoever abides in me and I in him, he it is that bears much fruit, for apart from me you can do nothing" (John 15:4-5 ESV).

What a great analogy that Jesus paints for us. Bearing fruit is the equivalent of being successful, whole, complete, and useful. But to get that you must abide. Abiding isn't a one-time thing, it's a continuous thing. It takes enduring. Some seasons of drought, storms or unfertile soil may hit us. Some seasons of plenty with abundance follow as well. Either way, you stay connected to the source, knowing that you don't toil for nothing, and that there will be a plentiful harvest. People around you see the fruit. Especially during a tough season when your joy continues to flow out of you and overflow to others.

Not abiding comes with a strict warning: "If anyone does not abide in me, he is thrown away like a branch and withers; and the branches are gathered, thrown into the fire, and burned" (John 15:6 ESV). Trees that don't bear fruit get cut down. There is no need for them. No purpose. Even something as simple and useful as shade doesn't come from a dead tree.

But with every strict warning of disobedience, comes an exciting promise of obedience: "If you abide in me, and my words abide in you, ask whatever you wish, and it will be done for you" (John 15:7 ESV). The crazy thing is, that if you are abiding, your priorities change. What you wanted and wished for when living in disobedience are the opposite of what you tend to wish for when you are abiding. Your selfish requests are now "others-focused". Your hopes and dreams are now God's hopes and dreams. When that transformative thinking takes root, whatever you wish will be done for you.

The result follows immediately: "By this my Father is glorified, that you bear much fruit and so prove to be my disciples" (John 15:8 ESV). Jesus's goal on Earth was to do the will of the Father. That should also be our goal as well. If we abide, our priorities change and we focus on our God given purpose in life, which ultimately is to glorify the Father. People around us see the change and that the fruit we have is so sweet that they want some of it, so they ask you. Now you are able to tell them what Jesus has done and is doing in your life now that you gave up control. They can't change your story, because it's your story.

Jesus continues with this statement: "As the Father has loved me, so have I loved you. Abide in my love. If you keep my commandments, you will abide in my love, just as I have kept my Father's commandments abide in his love" (John 15: 9-10 ESV). Jesus now relates abiding to love. If you truly love Jesus, you will abide. No matter the cost. No matter what you have to give up. No matter if you lose some friendships or that next promotion at work.

The outcome comes in the next verse and is at the end of the day, what we are all seeking: "These things I have spoken to you, that my joy may be in you, and that your joy may be full" (John 15:11 ESV). Joy is a state of mind. It's in your heart. It's not based on circumstances or the weather. You have joy regardless of what is going on around you or what the diagnosis is.

Dadvoted reader, I hope you don't just see the goodness of abiding, but that you are experiencing it. When you are abiding and walking in God's path for your life, it is so rich. This comes with a warning label though. The enemy won't like this and will attempt to thwart you. Be aware. Attack him with truth. Remember who wins in the end! "For our light and momentary troubles are achieving for us an eternal glory that far outweighs them all. So we fix our eyes not on what is seen, but on what is unseen, since what is seen is temporary, but what is unseen is eternal" (2 Corinthians 4:17-18). Abide or Die!

THAT ONE THING

WE ALL HAVE that *One Thing*. That one thing that is holding us back from reaching our full potential in Christ. If you regularly attend church, that *One Thing* is probably on your heart most Sunday mornings when the message is concluding, and the pastor closes in prayer. If attending a biblical based church that doesn't just bring the "feel good" message, you are hopefully convicted on Sunday and challenged as you leave feeling renewed and redirected. This is often not the case as many men feel condemned, which is from the enemy. They feel trapped. They hold it in because "men" do that. They isolate which allows the condemnation to grow as the guilt and shame are nurtured in isolation. This is a vicious cycle that unfortunately us men allow to happen for years and even decades. Our "toughness" and "muscle through" mentalities get in the way of us opening up and seeking healing which leads to freedom. The enemy loves these traits that were passed down from generation to generation which keeps a lot of men in bondage. As you read this, that *One Thing* is probably on your mind right now. What is it? What stronghold keeps you from reaching your full potential? What is suffocating you from being the dad, husband, leader, and man in the marketplace that you were called to be? What are you doing in secret that would embarrass you if your mom found out, let alone your spouse? Dadvoted man reading this, we've got to release this and we are going to start today!

I'm going to list a handful of things in hopes to bring these to light. Some strongholds or things that could be holding you back that come to mind are:

- Pride
- Addiction – alcohol, drugs, prescription pills, gambling, tobacco
- Unforgiveness
- Porn
- Your Friends
- Fear and Anxiety
- Laziness
- Lack of self-care
- Anger
- Trust Issues
- Lying
- Cheating on your taxes
- Emotional relationship with someone of the opposite sex
- Need for control
- Lust
- Depression
- Affair
- People-Pleasing

Let me also put the disclaimer out there that if I didn't list your struggle above, you don't get a hall pass. You know the *One Thing* that is holding you back. Own up to it and face it head on.

God can take these away and wants to intervene. He can flood your soul and take these urges away. Sometimes His intervention is immediate and sometimes it takes time; sometimes you can achieve victory without seeking medical help or counseling, or sometimes you might need the help of others. I am speaking from experience from both sides. I dipped for about 10 years from early in high school up until my mid-twenties. I stopped a few years after getting married as part of one of my commitments to Keeli. As I started a new career and traveled a lot, I started up the awful habit again without her knowing. I had a secret storage spot in my car and would drive 100 yards away from the house and stop and open the back hatch to get my stash out. She would ask here and there and one time she even smelt it on me; which resulted in me lying, which she believed. I would run bogus errands just to get a quick dip in. You may be thinking that tobacco use isn't the worst thing. It could be a lot worse. From a health perspective, it was bad and extremely addictive. But what ate at me the worst was my lying to Keeli. We were newly married and struggling financially. I would keep extreme tabs on her spending yet was spending $75 or so each month on this habit. This habit also led me down the path of other sins. I would be in a hotel room and instead of going to bed, I would stay up, turn the TV on and dip. At times, that would cause me to scroll through the hotel channels often times finding something to watch that was borderline inappropriate, or just flat out inappropriate. I wouldn't get but a few bad hours of sleep and would wake up feeling shame and sick. It was ongoing and was keeping me from being the best husband and employee. I'd still go to church on Sunday and loved Jesus, but it had me. Finally, one evening, I was reading the book *Crazy Love* by Francis Chan, and I was convicted to tell her the truth. I sat her down and told her everything. Like you may have thought earlier, she thought I was bringing something much worse to light and was relieved that it was just my admitting of this bad habit. She forgave me immediately. God removed this majorly addictive behavior on the spot. I threw away my can of tobacco and to this day have never even thought about it. Praise God!

The flipside to this story has been my use and abuse of alcohol over the past 20 plus years. Drinking was a part of my life from high school, college, early in my career and through early parenting. I was very cognizant of this habit in my mid-twenties and early thirties, as I led a high school guys groups for eight years and had to hold myself accountable. As the stresses of life hit, with a challenging career change and just life in general, drinking came back into play more and more. My two-to-three drink limit became limitless, which led to a stronger tolerance. Drinking was considered an escape, but also a means to celebrate or to unwind after a tough day, meaning everyday had a valid reason (in my mind) to have a drink. I was the "fun guy" at the party, at the work event, or on the golf course. I rallied people to "get after it" and have fun as we all deserve to have fun. Behind closed doors, I would pray for the desires to go away, often praying that God would make it taste bad so I could stop. I would often think, "when will this get old?" Then I would see people in their 60's and 70's drinking daily and that it never got old. It was a stronghold. In 2020, the Lord called me to write for the Kingdom. I was inspired. I pressed in and somewhat started, but where would I find the time? I work, I parent, I drink, and I sleep. Weekends are made for escaping, so you drink more. When was my time to pursue what God had placed on my heart? Keeli could only challenge me so much and she is my spouse, not my accountability partner. Also, my accountability guys are busy, and I could avoid them if I wanted to. One day, God spoke through a guy at my office and challenged me with the two toughest questions I've ever been asked:

1. "Are you hot or are you cold, Kevin? Or are you Lukewarm?"
2. "Are you fully living to please the Lord?"

Wow! What sobering questions (no pun intended). I speak to question one more in the topic titled L^5, but this is regarding how Jesus would rather us be not about Him at all versus being a little about Him and a little about the world, teetering between both. The second question prompted him to then ask me what was holding me back, which I admitted was alcohol. He challenged me to consider quitting mainly for the sake of my kids and their future so they wouldn't go down a similar path I was on. This was a concern for me and really for Keeli, but I never considered fully quitting. What would people think of me? So, a few more months went by of me being more aware but making no drastic changes. This was not an admit and be healed immediately like what I spoke about above, because I wasn't ready to admit that I needed help. Finally, I decided to half-heartedly seek out a recovery group at our Church called Regeneration. This group is for people with all types of struggles (a lot of what is listed above) who are willing to seek Jesus for ultimate healing and recovery. I was very skeptical but had heard some amazing stories over the past few years and always had an inkling in my mind to show up. Once I did, I realized that this was the game changer I needed. I can now admit the stronghold of alcohol has been released and now I am living my fullest for Jesus and for the Kingdom! The freedom that I have witnessed is so refreshing. My anxieties have ceased, I am more productive, and I feel amazing. The list could go on and on about how this was the best decision I've ever made. *Thank you, Lord, for speaking through Antoine, and challenging me to change for myself, my family and for Your purposes! Thank You for recovery programs like Regeneration that were created by people who love You and needed real recovery.*

Dadvoted reader, I could easily not share this about me and hide behind the computer screen telling you what you should or shouldn't do, but that's not real life. Real life is about being vulnerable, partnering with God and others for help, and seeing miracles happen in front of you. I hope my story encourages you to do the same with your struggles or strongholds. But there comes a caveat. You can't just speak it and will it to come to existence. Getting out of the darkness requires action. Physical action. You must walk from the darkness into the light. The first part is confession. This is not something most men are equipped to do. We were taught that being vulnerable means that you are weak. It is actually the opposite of being weak and is another tactic the enemy has engrained in men for generations. The Bible says in James 5:16, "Therefore confess your sins to each other and pray for each other so that you may be healed. The prayer of a righteous person is powerful and effective."

Too many men are stuck in a rut. If you ever have had your car or truck stuck in a rut, it can be a scary feeling. I remember getting my Explorer stuck in the mud in the middle of nowhere in high school while fishing with my best friend Brian. It was dusk and before the age of cellphones. We were in a bind and close to having to sleep all night in woods—this was not a good feeling at all. Thankfully, we found the last truck leaving the area and they were able to pull us out. That's also what confession is all about. It's the start of getting someone to help pull you out of the rut. It's often the push and pull scenario that we run into as men. We have a lot of people who care about us and are pushing us to be better, like your wife, parents, in-laws, kids and so on. But so often we dig in and the pushing does nothing or makes us dig in all the more depending on how stubborn we are. When we finally come to grips and see that we need help, we reach out a hand and ask people to pull us out of the rut. Then change begins to happen.

The first step of action is on you Dadvoted reader. You have to want to change. You have to see that your actions or mindset is creating the setback or stronghold in your family, relationships and is affecting your kids or their futures. From there you must seek help. Recovery groups through the church do some of the most powerful ministry that we very seldom hear about. Start there. Many churches also have counseling that is free or of little charge. And of course, you can consult a pastor to give you resources. I also have to say here that breaking some addictions will require medical assistance or monitoring, so I do not recommend going cold turkey trying to quit on any substance you have been putting in your body for years. You need to consult a medical advisor.

We all have the *One Thing* that holds us back. I had it, and it had to come to head and had to be released. I'm just thankful I didn't physically cause any major harm to anyone or to my family. Seek help! Don't think you got this on your own. Do it for yourself, do it for your kids, do it for your marriage, do it to become alive and thriving in God's purpose for your life.

> *Lord, I pray over this reader who is reading this right now. He has committed to reading this book so that he can become a better dad, a devoted dad, Dadvoted. We are so thankful that You hear our cries for help and that You don't give up on Your people that love You, seek You, and fear You. That there is nothing we can do for You to love us any less. That You saved us all, so we can live a life of purpose to advance Your Kingdom and lead our families so they can also advance Your Kingdom. This reader knows right now what that One Thing that is holding him back from being "all in" and fully living for You. My prayer is that Your Spirit would speak to him right now and he would be convicted to get help. That he could confess what he*

has been doing in secret and that You would provide the correct means of recovery to begin the healing process. Lord, where the enemy is present or is creeping into this reader's thoughts, I ask that he would depart immediately. The stakes are too high. He is tired of being stuck in a rut and we need You to do what only You can do and take away this stronghold. His kids need him to be released from this, his wife needs it, and You are ready to reveal something new to him that will change his course and direction. I pray for forgiveness over the stubbornness us men have been taught and I pray that this reader would accept Your healing power. You are so good and we know that You are working, moving and removing strongholds to free Your people to live fully for You. In Your precious name we pray, Amen!

MIRROR IMAGES

I **RECENTLY RAN** across a powerful European commercial on LinkedIn that had several scenes with adults doing outrageous acts while their young child followed suit, mimicking the same activity in their childish form right behind them. They were the adult's shadow. They were a mirror image of the adult "in charge." There were a handful of scenes, but three stood out to me.

1. Dad road rage – Dad was in the car yelling and throwing his hands up at other drivers. The kid in the backseat was probably five-years-old and was mocking him and flipping the bird out the window passionately with both hands.

2. Dad walking past a lady in disgust – An elderly lady was blocking the escalator as her hands were full and she clearly needed help. The dad looked down at her as if she was a peasant and an inconvenience to him by being in the way. His son walked right by her and glared at her eye level as if saying "how dare you be in my way!"

3. Dad abusing mom – The dad was standing over a mom in the fetal position yelling at her while the son mimicked every move almost in sync. At the end the dad raised his fist to hit the mom and the camera panned over to her view and it was the little boy

standing over his mom with raised fist. This was no doubt the most disturbing of all.

I saw this public service announcement only once and have not been able to find it again, knowing that it's probably too real, intense and risqué for the American mainstream media to grasp (though anything sexual is at the forefront of what we view). I know that some of these examples may seem extreme, but little eyes are watching every move you make. How you act and react will be embedded in your kids. Your kids have a choice, to either follow your ways or to run from your ways. You would think it would be easy, but it's not. So many kids grow up and emulate the activities they learned from their fathers even if they see and experience the consequences and harmful outcomes.

I spoke on generational sin earlier and this is an extension of that concept as well. Dadvoted reader, what do you want to pass along to your kids? It doesn't have to just be blatant, extremely harmful things that you pass along to your kids, but it can be subtle social and lifestyle choices as well. Do you talk trash about people immediately after they walk away or after you leave a family outing, and your kids are in the back of the car hearing every word you say? Are you negative or pessimistic? Do you help around the house, or let your wife run ragged? Do you casually cuss around your neighbors or on the phone with coworkers when your kids are around? Do you have a habit that you can't quit?

What about spiritually? Do you choose to worship every Sunday and make church a priority if you are in town? Are you setting aside time to pray with your kids and do devotionals with them? Do they know that you love Jesus? Do you have Deuteronomy 6: 6-9 as a family motto in your heart? "These commandments that I give you today are to be on your hearts. Impress them on your children. Talk about them when you sit at home and when you walk along the road, when you lie down and when you get up. Tie them as symbols on your hands and bind them on your foreheads. Write them on the doorframes of your houses and on your gates." I say this often, but we control the narrative in our house and in our kids. But more importantly we are giving them a roadmap for life based on how we act. They are watching every move you make. I think this poem by Edgar Guest solidifies my thoughts:

"There are little eyes upon you and they're watching night and day.
There are little ears that quickly take in every word you say.
There are little hands all eager to do anything you do;
And a little boy who's dreaming of the day he'll be like you.
You're the little fellow's idol, you're the wisest of the wise.
In his little mind about you no suspicions ever rise.
He believes in you devoutly, holds all you say and do;
He will say and do, in your way when he's grown up just like you.
There's a wide-eyed little fellow who believes you're always right;
And his eyes are always opened, and he watches day and night.
You are setting an example every day in all you do;
For the little boys who's waiting to grow up to be like you."

What a touching poem and reminder for all us dads. I also remember the old country song by Rodney Atkins called "Watching You." I recommend you look that up on YouTube. We have so much influence over our kids, and we unfortunately forget this at times or don't understand the magnitude. This poem pointed more towards raising boys, but if you are a girl dad, your role is extremely vital as well. For what you are teaching your daughter, by your example, is how a man loves. Hopefully you show that he is tender. Hopefully you demonstrate how he treats people well and respects women.

One day when she starts dating, she is going to most likely look for a man who embodies the same characteristics as you. You better make those shoes hard to fill!

Dadvoted reader, I know your heart; you want to raise your kids in a safe and secure environment and to guide them in life. What you do and say is being watched closely. That could appear to be a lot of pressure and there is no doubt pressure on you. If you have been brash and quick tempered, it's never too late to apologize and start over. If you have had a tendency to be negative, or talk about people, repent, admit and talk to your kids about your struggles. You don't have to pretend like you got it all together (because you don't). If you haven't been present, even when you are at home, change today. Your shadow will one day become your mirror image!

ROOTED AND GROUNDED

I **WANT TO** pause as we get closer here to let you know that I have complete confidence in you! If you've made it this far, you have a firm foundation established, you are convicted of change you may need to pursue, and you are charged with the tools to continue your journey of Dadvotedness. My personal challenge is that you implement something you have found useful. My prayer for you comes specifically from Ephesians 3: 14-19 (ESV), as Paul says it better than I ever could:

"For this reason I bow my knees before the Father, from whom every family in heaven and on earth is named, that according to the riches of his glory he may grant you to be strengthened with power through his Spirit in your inner being, so that Christ may dwell in your hearts through faith – that you, being underline rooted and grounded in love, may have strength to comprehend with all the saints what is the breadth and length and height and depth, and to know the love of Christ that surpasses knowledge, that you may be filled with all the fullness of God."

You are rooted. Rooted to face the storms. Rooted to dig deeper to find water during seasons of drought. Rooted so that the winds of life, uncertainty and disappointment don't sway you to be uprooted. Rooted in rich soil. You are strong. A branch may break here and there, but your roots are never disturbed. You know who you are and whose you are. You flourish when the world says you shouldn't and it confuses them. Your fruit is apparent. All those around you are changed or challenged.

You are grounded. You have a firm foundation. You are secure in your walk and established in your thoughts. You are confident in your core, but more confident in the Creator. Nothing moves you. Waves may crash into you, but you are unshakeable. You want others to have what you have, so you are vocal; not condemning but living out your testimony.

You are rooted and grounded in love. Christ's love consumes you. You know that you were bought with a price. God's spirit lives in you which changes everything. You have a love affair with Jesus. He is the author and perfector of your faith. The fruits of the Spirit are apparent in you. Your old ways are gone. Your eyes are pointed forward. Your path is God's path. This love surpasses knowledge. And you are filled with fullness. That only comes from God.

Dadvoted reader, I've been rooting for you to be grounded all along. A lot of people have been rooting for me to be grounded as well and I bet you have the same following. It's been a journey, but it's so worth it. As we transition to our final two charges, let's never forget how God has shown up. That He never gives up on His people. Pass this along. Others need to know. Stay the course.

As MEN, WE are programmed in many ways. Working hard to provide is most likely a key character trait all men have and is a driving force in many of us. This is a good thing and is biblical in nature, but it is only a small fraction of our life's worth. Where does your legacy fall into the grand scheme of things? Do you think about it? Should you be thinking about it? It would probably be safe to say that through the early and middle stages of our life that we don't think about it at all. I can attest to that as I just hit my 40's. I wake up, I work, I parent, I go, go, go and then I crash. Rinse and repeat day after day and week after week. Life is busy and we just roll with the punches. Today's challenge is to take a step back, take a deep breath, and consider your legacy right now. If you died today, what would your kids say? What would your spouse say about you? What would your friends and coworkers say about you? I certainly hope that "hard worker" and "good provider" wouldn't be the theme of your funeral. That would be sad and surfacy to say the least. And the hardest question of all would be, "What would the Lord say about you?" Did you fulfill the mission He put you here to do? Did you love as He called you to love? Sobering thoughts to say the least. Some of you may have solid answers and don't have much soul searching to do here, and I applaud you big time. Keep up the good work and stay the course. You are on the path to reaching your full Dadvoted potential! Now to the rest of us, we may need a reset and that's OK. Resets are good and often needed. I had a reset this year when I realized that alcohol was creeping too much into my life and was holding me back from reaching my full potential for the Lord, my family, my ministry, and my career. I joined a men's recovery group through the church and increased my accountability 100-fold. This was the best decision I've ever made and was necessary to catapult me into God's full plan for my life. So how do we reset and get back on track to living a life of substance that will leave a lasting legacy?

When contemplating legacy, I had to slow down, self-evaluate, and realign my thoughts by asking the following questions, and I challenge you to do the same. Do I truly care about people? Ouch! Am I genuine and do I genuinely care about people, or do I have tendencies to live on the surface or just try to impress people? Do I listen well to people, or am I just thinking about how I am going to respond back, missing what they were saying? When I meet someone and they tell me their name do I remember it, or do I forget it instantly? Am I ever trying to compare myself to others? Am I trying to appear that I have it all together all the time? Do I keep up with friends and foster authentic relationships? When was the last time I laughed so hard that my abs (or as my kids call them "flabs") hurt the next day? Am I leading my family? Am I teaching my boys to care about people, all people, even the difficult ones? Am I using my God given talents efficiently? Am I using my God given identity in a meaningful way? Am I consistently learning new things, challenging myself, and stepping out of my comfort zone? Are people better off because of me or do I use people to make my life better? And finally, do I love people. Do I love my wife how I should? Do I relentlessly love my boys? Do I give them my best? Do I love people and put their needs before my own?

L^5 is rooted from the questions above. The big "L" stands for Legacy. The number 5 is the exponent (you may have to dig deep into middle school math), or better pronounced L to the 5th power. The 5 L's that I deem essential to living a life of substance and leaving behind a lasting legacy are **Lead, Laugh, Love, Learn and Listen**. Yes, these are all basic words, but these 5 action verbs are exponentially supercharged when the **Lord** is in the center of your life. We are going to break these down and then talk about the opposite of L to the 5th power.

The 5 L's

Lead – We are all leaders! It doesn't matter your job title or your age. It doesn't matter if you are the president of a major corporation or a line worker in a plant; if you are 25 or if you are 85. You are a leader, and you are meant to lead! You are a leader at home. The tone is set by you in your household. Your spouse and you partner together, but you are the head of the house. You set the direction of your family both emotionally and spiritually. Leaders are always present and bring 100% energy and effort when at home. Call your kids to lead and engrain it in them to challenge them to step up at school and in their after-school activities. In the marketplace, you may or may not lead a team or have the title of manager, but you are a leader. You lead by example: doing the right things, working hard, not complaining but encouraging the people around you. People know you are different, but they can't quite figure out why initially. You are a servant leader. You don't ask anyone to do anything you wouldn't do yourself. You do jobs and tasks that aren't technically part of your title (i.e., take out the trash, or help when short staffed), because you care about the people around you. Finally, you lead people to Jesus. Your words and actions portray that you are grounded and you live differently. You aren't self-centered. When they ask why you are how you are, you point them to Jesus. You have a testimony about what God has done in your life that challenges them to think about their faith and potentially pursue Christ. You speak in truth with love.

Laugh – "Laughter is the best medicine." When people are around you, you make them feel good. Not only because you encourage and compliment them, but because you make them laugh. This is natural for you regardless of your personality or if you are introverted. Don't think that you can't relate to people or bring a smile to someone's face. This isn't forced, but is genuinely who you are. You don't try or appear to be something you are not. You are comfortable in your own skin. You laugh at yourself. You don't take yourself so seriously and find humor in the silly things you do or say. You joke with your kids. There is so much happiness in your household because you set the tone. You use sarcasm sparingly and know when your light prodding is getting borderline to hurting someone's feelings. You draw a deep sense of Joy from Jesus, who enjoys when we laugh, cut up and have fun. He wired us this way.

Love – You love big. Your kids know that you love them because you tell them often and you show them that you do by being present. You love your wife in public. You still have the same fervor for her that you had when you started dating. Your kids see that love and, though they may think its gross, it doesn't stop you from kissing her, embracing her and maybe even giving her a little pat on the butt. She's your prize and your angel. You are intentional in all your relationships. You keep up with people. You pray for people often and you tell them that you are doing so. You see the greatness in people, and you challenge them to reach that level of greatness that you see in them. You praise in public and correct in private. You still believe in the handwritten thank you note knowing that people keep these and often refer back to them. You love Jesus. He is at the core of you. You meet with Him daily and talk to Him throughout the day. His love flows to and through you.

Learn – You take learning seriously, knowing that you are either getting better or moving backwards. Regardless of your age, you are willing to learn something new. You seek wisdom and knowledge through scripture and other sources. You lean on learning from others and are never too good to have someone show you something. You learn from your mistakes and bad decisions. You use those moments to teach others so that they don't make the same errors that you made. You learn and lean into Jesus for everything and work to model how He lived and taught. You learn that you are a disciple and how to disciple others so you can pass along the ways of Christ. Retirement isn't your main career goal, but honoring Jesus throughout your whole life and seeking His wisdom is your guiding light and ultimate goal.

Listen – Hearing and listening aren't the same thing. I hear lots of things throughout the day, but listening is an active task that requires both your ears and your eyes. You engage in active listening because you care about the person speaking more than all the other distractions around you. Your phone stays on silent and you dare not look at it while someone is talking to you. You ask follow-up questions and are curious about the other person speaking. You listen to your kids after your long day of work and don't just generically ask them about their day. Again, you engage! You get on their level and regardless of how random their story is, you listen to it. You set time aside weekly to catch up with your wife so you are on her page and can listen to her needs and share yours as well. Lack of communication is such the root of so many problems in work, marriages and at home and you are fully aware of this. Finally, you listen to Jesus. He can speak to you in so many ways, but you are always listening to His spirit for guidance, direction, and/or movement. You have a spirit of expectancy knowing that He is going to speak, so you are all the more aware.

Now that we covered L^5, let's review what it is not. L to the 5th power has a reversal to it, or L to the negative 5th power written L^{-5}. This is unfortunately the opposite of living a life of substance and leaving a legacy. In the center of it is Lucifer, or the devil. This enemy doesn't want us to live for the Lord and leave a lasting legacy. He wants us to live for ourselves and desires on earth without an eternal mindset. He wants to speak against our identity in God and set up false roadblocks in our minds that cause us to freeze and not pursue what the Lord set us on Earth to do. The crazy thing about it is that it isn't all blatantly big and bad rebellion against the Lord or us physically worshipping the devil. L^{-5} can take many forms for believers and nonbelievers alike and be on either end of the spectrum from moral to immoral in the case of thoughts, motives, and actions. God wants to advance the Kingdom with His people where the enemy wants us to be stagnant and just live comfortable. God wants us to live fearlessly, the enemy wants us to live in fear. God wants to use our past mistakes to grow further in Him and live in His redeeming love. The enemy wants us to be stuck in our shame and guilt.

Traits of L^{-5} or L to the negative 5th power:

Lust – We normally talk about lusting in sexual terms, but it can also be described as a strong desire for something. This can be riches, power, fame, food, to be known, etc. When you lust for something, it is about filling a desire for yourself and will most often leave you feeling sick or not satisfied once you obtain it. When we lust for something that is not in God's will for our life it becomes an idol. God is very firm about idols and His hate for idolatry. God is a jealous God and doesn't want anything to be sought after more than Him. Exodus 3:3 states God's first commandment to us; "You shall have no other gods before me." When we prop something else up in our mind and strive with all we have to obtain it, that idol becomes our god, and we push the Living God off to the side. You can't leave a lasting legacy if you lust for the things of the world. Yes, you may end up successful and may reach the riches and fame that you wanted, but at what cost. Mark 8:36 says; "What good is it for someone to gain the whole world, yet forfeit their soul?" Your family may call you "good provider," but all that money left will be spent or used to obtain more worldly pleasures. If your desire is to leave a lasting legacy, then you must lust for the things of God.

Leaning on Self – Legacy builders are self*less* not self*ish*. Those that seek only what's good for them are stuck in a trap and thinking the world revolves around them. Especially if a fancy title follows your name, a feeling that you have "made it" in life can creep in and you are more prone to have it be all about you. Your way and your will overtake God's way and His will. This trap ensnares so many men. Look, I get it. You've worked hard, you've earned this, you had to pay your dues. Kingdom men and legacy builders don't fall into this trap. They are grateful of the path and success that the Lord gave them. They want to see others succeed and want to pass along that knowledge to see others do well and not make many of the same mistakes. When you become less about you and more about others those building blocks of your legacy stack high to build a strong, firm and tall foundation.

Liar – I'm not labeling you a liar; instead, I would label you a believer of lies. If you are stuck in L^{-5}, you are believing a lie somewhere inside about yourself. It could be something that was spoken over you as a child or someway the enemy is twisting or manipulating your true identity. False identities that cause us to freeze, be inactive, or cause us to fear is one of the enemy's main tasks to keep us inactive. You must understand and know your identity and silence the enemy. I highly recommend you read the book *Living Fearless* by Jamie Winship to uncover God's identity for you and to remove the false identity that may have taken root. He speaks a lot about the enemy and his deception. He also talks about defeating the enemy with truth. Below is an excerpt from his book:

"Satan is not fearful of us memorizing verses. He quotes verses to deceive us. Likewise, Satan is not afraid of the Bible itself. We're sleeping with the Bible or waving the book at Satan and shouting, "Go away, Satan." He's not afraid of this.

What Satan fears is truth. He can't tolerate truth or truth tellers. That's how Jesus beats him every time. Jesus speaks only truth to the Liar, and the Liar can speak only deception back. Deception cannot exist in the place where truth shines." (Winship, 2022)[12]

Dadvoted reader, we must uncover the lies of the enemy and attack them with truth. You are a child of the Most High God! Created to do good works (Ephesians 2:10). Set apart and appointed (Jeremiah 1:5). Your time is now!

Loathing – Those with hate in their heart towards anyone or anything will have a tough road to building a lasting legacy. Today, more than ever, I feel that there is so much hate and dissension in this world. Our country is divided. Political seats and stances seem to determine our attitudes these days. Social media only fuels the fire even more as the extreme left and the extreme right, which are very small in %, are the loudest behind the postings. This is only fueling more hate and uncertainty. Do we men of faith not believe that God is in control? That He allows these leaders into office? That He will work all things for good? That in the end He will reign forever and none of this will mean anything? The only hate I will ever promote is that you hate <u>your own</u> sin. Not someone else's sin, but your own sin, period! If you live with any ounce of hate or extreme negativity in your heart, one of 2 things will accompany your legacy: 1. Those in your watch will follow your ways. 2. Those in your watch will avoid you as much as possible.

Lukewarm – This may be the enemy's favorite trait of L^{-5}. He loves it because it's a place of complacency. You are probably morally good, but not a threat to push past the darkness and advance the Kingdom. If you are lukewarm, you aren't' all in for anything, especially the things of God. In Revelation 3:15 the church of Laodicea gets a tough warning: "I know your deeds, that you are neither cold nor hot. I wish you were either one or the other! So, because you are lukewarm – neither hot nor cold – I am about to spit you out of my mouth." Being lukewarm is a scary place to be and even more scary because you don't realize the implications of being in this state. You may proclaim some Jesus here and there. Show up on Sunday, shout an Amen once in a while and maybe even serve. But your heart still waivers back and forth from the worldly to the eternal things. You are wishy washy and not committed. Look, I'm not casting stones here. I'm the first to admit that I had lukewarm living down to a science. I served, I worshipped God, I had my quiet time, but would daily choose to live for myself and my pleasures over full obedience to God. I still have to make this choice daily and will for the rest of my life. Even key figures in the Bible, like King David forgot his identity and who he was in Christ later in life and he made very bad decisions and fell into some major traps. The good news is that God redeemed him and still called him "A man after God's own heart," and he can do the same for you. To break the cycle of lukewarmness, you need to go on the attack. You need to confess, phone a friend, connect with a men's group, and begin the process of complete transformation.

My biggest fear for the men of today is that they will be lifeless. They will be alive, but not living abundantly. They will have a sense of godliness, but not experience the full power (2 Timothy 3:5). The things of this world will choke them (Mark 4:19) from receiving what God has for them today. Dadvoted man, let's not have this be the case. Your legacy comes from the Lord. Don't let the world determine it. Do you want success or significance?

Let's transition back to the positive terms in L^5 and review the order they were put in:

- Lead
- Laugh
- **LOVE**
- Learn
- Listen

Lead, Laugh, Learn, Listen really aren't in any particular order, but the word Love is bold, underlined, and placed the middle for a reason. Love is at the center of L the 5th power, your legacy and everything else. I have to point to the famous love verse in Corinthians that we hear at most weddings. But before the most known portion of "love is patient, love is kind," I go to the beginning of the chapter that says; "If I speak in the tongues of men or of angels, but do not have love, I am only a resounding gong or a clanging cymbal. If I have the gift of prophecy and can fathom all mysteries and all knowledge, and if I have a faith that can move mountains, but do not have love, I am nothing. If I give all I possess to the poor and give over my body to hardship that I may boast, but do not have love, I gain nothing" (1 Cor 13: 1-3).

To summarize that verse and apply it, your legacy will be all for not if there was not love in you along the way. You can build your own kingdom, make a ton of money, or even do great things for the world, but if it's done without love you will gain nothing. You'll have a legacy, but not a lasting one that transcends generations. You may make the news, but days and months will go by, and people will move on. What are you leaving behind that will be passed down from generation to generation? Dadvoted reader, my hope is as follows: My hope is that every man would <u>Love</u> Jesus so much that every person he encounters is changed in some way forever. That the love of Christ would exude out of every man and that he would <u>Lead</u> his family and kids with gusto and enthusiasm. That we would have joy and happiness follow us as we <u>Laugh</u> our way through this short life we get on earth. That we would always be willing to <u>Learn</u> and never too old to take on a new challenge. And that we would not only <u>Listen</u> well to people, but that we would listen to the spirit of God in all things, all decisions, and all moments. If we follow this, our legacies will be lasting my friend. Let's start today!

STAND FIRM

THERE HAVE BEEN a ton of challenging questions asked in this book. Let me reiterate that these aren't one-sided or just me spewing challenges your way. I am constantly asking myself these same questions and am in the throes of the battle with you on obtaining ultimate Dadvotedness. As we close though, I have a few more to ask. For us to ponder and commit to in order to shift the mindset and the culture of dads.

1. Are you a fair-weather fan or are you a fanatic?
2. Are you a spectator or a starter?
3. Are you ordinary or extraordinary?
4. Are you on a cruise ship or a battleship?

Fair-weather fans like a team only when they are winning. When it's easy to love them. When all the puzzle pieces are put together and everything is flowing in unison. Fanatics are loyal. They love the team and stand by the team regardless of the record and regardless of what others think. They are fanatical! They paint their face and show up in negative temperatures to root on their team. In victory or defeat they keep their head up. So much is the same for the spiritual life. Are you a fair-weather fan? Do you only love Jesus when all is going your way? When your bank account is booming and the stock market is soaring? When your life is rolling along like

Burger King and you have everything "Your Way?" You avoid pursuing Kingdom things because you are content with being comfortable. Why stir up the enemy when you have it going good over here? We need more fanatics for Jesus; fanatics who are willing to put everything on the line for Him. We need fanatics to seek and serve and live out our purpose; to keep our head held up when the enemy takes a slight lead or we get spiritually injured. I think you know the answer here. Dadvoted reader, you are so close to crossing over here. Take that step. It's refreshing and rewarding.

Spectators sit in the stands and watch the game. They don't put in the work or have the skillset to play the game at the highest level. They certainly can talk a good game, but they have no game. Once the game is over, they move on with life. Starters, on the other hand, are committed. They put in the work and the extra work to achieve greatness. They live and breathe the game that consumes them. Victories are sweet but defeat causes growth. They play for the team not the individual. The same goes for the spiritual life. Are you a spectator or a starter? Are you on God's team or just watching from a distance? Do you wake up daily ready to be used? Or are you spiritually sidelined? Get in the game! You are equipped and ready to play under Christ's coaching.

Ordinary people are everywhere. Their life is mundane with no adventure or action. They live a life of daily repetitiveness: work, parent, sleep, repeat. They live for the weekend. They are bored. Extraordinary people live for excitement. They expect great things to happen, and they want to be in the center of it. "Status quo, more like status no" is how they view life. Why do things the same? Just because we've always done it that way? Wrong answer. There is always a new way. A more innovative way. Do you want to live an ordinary spiritual life or extraordinary spiritual life? The ordinary revolves around Sunday church and maybe a Wednesday here and there. Maybe you are in a community group, but you just go because your wife forces you. Dadvoted reader, there is so much more! Extraordinary spiritual living is partnering with Jesus and it's active, not stagnant. You live expecting God to move, and guess what? He does. He moves subtly in your heart and sometimes massively in public. Your faith is strengthened either way. You clear all the noise to hear from the King. You don't think religion and rules, you have a relationship with the Creator. You pray passionately asking Heaven to invade Earth. We can't take this lightly. This is too good! Why be ordinary when you can be extraordinary?

Is your life comparable to being on a cruise ship or on a battleship? Do you wake up every day with little-to-no purpose other than to make a paycheck and be a good person? Or when you wake up do your feet hit the floor knowing that you are going to war? War against the enemy, war to protect your kids and marriage, war to protect your mind. Are you a partner with Christ to advance His Kingdom? Does the enemy shutter when your feet hit the ground each morning? We are in a battle, but seldom do we know or acknowledge it. How do we stay the course? How do we keep our passion and fervor in such a fallen world? Dadvoted reader, we must **Stand Firm!**

Bear with me here and really read all these scriptures below, showing how the Bible is emphatic about us standing firm.

> "**Stand firm**, and you will win life." Luke 21:19

> "They are brought to their knees and fall, but we rise up and **stand firm**." Psalms 20:8

> "Your statutes, Lord, **stand firm**; holiness adorns your house for endless days." Psalms 93:5

"Your word, Lord, is eternal; it **stands firm** in the heavens." Psalms 119:89

"When the storm has swept by, the wicked are gone, but the righteous **stand firm** forever." Proverbs 10:25

"The wicked are overthrown and are no more, but the house of the righteous **stands firm**." Proverbs 12:7

"Because of the increase of wickedness, the love of most will grow cold, but the one who **stands firm** to the end will be saved." Matt 24: 12-13

"Be on your guard; **stand firm** in the faith; be courageous; be strong." 1 Corinthians 16:13

"You too, be patient and **stand firm**, because the Lord's coming is near." James 5:8

"**Stand firm** then, with the belt of truth buckled around your waist, with the breastplate of righteousness in place," Ephesians 6:14

"Yet if you devote your heart to him and stretch out your hands to him, if you put away the sin that is in your hand and allow no evil to dwell in your tent, then, free of fault, you will lift up your face; you will **stand firm** and without fear." Job 11: 13-15

"But the plans of the Lord **stand firm** forever, the purposes of his heart through all generations." Psalms 33:11

"I will declare that your love **stands firm** forever, that you have established your faithfulness in heaven itself." Psalms 89:2

"Everyone will hate you because of me, but the one who **stands firm** to the end will be saved." Mark 13:13

"Now it is God who makes both us and you **stand firm** in Christ. He anointed us," 2 Corinthians 1:21

"You will be hated by everyone because of me, but the one who **stands firm** to the end will be saved." Matthew 10:22

"Not that we lord it over your faith, but we work with you for your joy, because it is by faith you **stand firm**." 2 Corinthians 1:24

"It is for freedom that Christ has set us free. **Stand firm**, then, and do not let yourselves be burdened again by a yoke of slavery." Galatians 5:1

"Therefore, my brothers and sisters, you whom I love and long for, my joy and crown, **stand firm** in the Lord in this way, dear friends." Philippians 4:1

"So then, brothers and sisters, **stand firm** and hold fast to the teachings we passed on to you, whether by word of mouth or by letter." 2 Thessalonians 2:15

"If you do not **stand firm** in your faith, you will not stand at all." Isaiah 7:9b

"Moses answered the people, "Do not be afraid. **Stand firm** and you will see the deliverance the Lord will bring you today." Exodus 14:13

"Therefore, my dear brothers and sisters, **stand firm**. Let nothing move you. Always give yourselves fully to the work of the Lord." 1 Corinthians 15:58

"Epaphras, who is one of you and a servant of Christ Jesus, sends greetings. He is always wrestling in prayer for you, that you may **stand firm** in all the will of God, mature and fully assured." Colossians 4:12

"Nevertheless, God's solid foundation **stands firm**, sealed with this inscription: "The Lord knows those who are his," and, "Everyone who confesses the name of the Lord must turn away from wickedness." 2 Timothy 2:19

"You will not have to fight this battle. Take up your positions: **stand firm** and see the deliverance the Lord will give you, Judah and Jerusalem. Do not be afraid: do not be discouraged. Go out and face

them tomorrow, and the Lord will be with you." 2
Chronicles 20:17

I know this list may feel exhausting, but what do you think the
Bible is emphasizing here? **Stand Firm!** Why do you think it is
listed 26 times? We are hardheaded. I think we should pay close
attention here. I think obedience is our only option. Let's look at
all the promises that follow if we stand firm:

- You will win life
- You will be mature and fully assured
- You will be delivered
- You will not be moved
- You won't have to fight the battle
- You won't fear or be discouraged
- The Lord will be with You
- You will rise up
- Holiness will adorn your house
- You will withstand the storms and the wicked
- You will be saved
- You will be prepared
- God's purposes will be passed from generation to generation
- You will be free of fault
- God's faithfulness will be established
- You will be anointed
- Joy will follow you
- You will have freedom
- The Word and teachings will be in your heart
- You will always work for the Lord
- You will turn from wickedness

Dadvoted man, let's make a declaration today to **Stand Firm** no matter what! No matter what is thrown at us. No matter what the world says we should or shouldn't do. No matter what others think or say. No matter what the medical report says. I'm tired of men being sissified and wussified! I'm tired of women being the spiritual head of our households. It is time to dig in and stand firm, leading our families and changing the course of this world for generations to come! You have the foundation built. It's strong. The cracks have been mended in Christ. You are solid. You can withstand anything. Any storm, trial or test. God is faithful. You have been redeemed! He has chosen you! God doesn't need you, but He wants you. All of you!

Declare today as Joshua did in the Old Testament that, "As for me and my house, we will serve the Lord." Now go serve the Lord!

NOTES

ENDNOTES

1   Oxford Dictionaries, staunch, Oxford Languages Dictionary. https://languages.oup.com

2   Oxford Dictionaries, fervent, Oxford Languages Dictionary. https://languages.oup.com

3   Tozer, A. W. (1978). The Knowledge of the Holy. Zondervan.

4   (2009, November 11). "Life without God is like an unsharpened pencil–it has no point." Diasover. from https://www.diasoverdiaries.wordpress.com/2009/11/11/

5   Evans, T. (2021). Kingdom Men Rising: A Call to Growth and Greater Influence. Bethany House Publishers, 69-70

6   Dweck, C. S. (2006). Mindset: The New Psychology of Success. Random House Digital, Inc.

7   Warren, R. (2002). The Purpose-driven Life: What on Earth Am I Here For? Zondervan.

8   Sloss, M. (2021, October 23). 15 Ridiculous Reasons Why People Got Complaints At Work. BuzzFeed. https://www.buzzfeed.com/morgansloss1/ridiculous-complaints-reddit

9   What is Grit? (n.d.). GoStrengths! https://www.gostrengths.com/what-is-grit/

10   Centers for Disease Control and Prevention (2022, May 17) https://www.cdc.gov/obesity/data/childhood.html

[11] Center for Humane Technology. (n.d.). https://www.human-etech.com/insights/60-minutes-social-media-and-political-polarization-in-america

[12] Winship, J. (2022). Living Fearless: Exchanging the Lies of the World for the Liberating Truth of God. Revell, 69.

ABOUT THE AUTHOR

KEVIN GOODNIGHT RESIDES in the suburbs of Houston with his wife Keeli, their two boys Keaton (12) and Kort (10), their dog Zoey and bunny Simba. They met their freshman year at Baylor University and lived in Sacramento for eight years before moving back to Texas in 2013. Kevin has made his career in the flooring industry in various leadership capacities and is currently the General Manager of Redi Carpet in Stafford, TX.

In 2020, Kevin's journaling turned into a calling to write, which morphed into a focus and passion for challenging Dads. The brand and LLC DADVOTED was created in 2022 and this book will be his first published piece, though he is currently working on two other writing projects. You can learn more by searching DADVOTED on all major social media sites or by going to www.dadvoted.com.

His heart is to challenge Dads to pursue what really matters in terms of authenticity, work/life balance and leaving a lasting legacy both in the home and in the marketplace. His dynamic personality and encouraging spirit coupled with vulnerability and transparency allow him to connect deeply with all people regardless of their stage of life.

When not working, writing or hauling kids to activities, Kevin enjoys working out, cooking, watching football and outdoor activities with his family including hiking, kayaking and jumping on the trampoline.

CPSIA information can be obtained
at www.ICGtesting.com
Printed in the USA
JSHW010818020523
40988JS00007B/6